Art of Magic

Art of Magic

Dr. Michael T. Mayo

Queens Army LLC   Tucson, Arizona

ISBN 978-1-7345741-2-8

E-book ISBN 978-1-7345741-4-2

Library of Congress Control Number: 2020910416

Published by: Queens Army LLC

2300 N. Craycroft Rd. #5

Tucson, Arizona 85712

Our website is: queensarmy.net

Pictures on front and back covers are courtesy of PIXABAY

Distributed by Ingram

Date of first printing, July 2020

Contents

Introduction to Art of Magic

The Source gave me the gift of magic. He said I would have to figure out how to use the magic on my own. He took me to a place in the Sonoran desert where there was a large sign that read, "The Art of Magic". On the opposite side of that sign it said, "Carnival of Magic." The "Carnival of Magic" had one hundred and seven concessions. The Source told me to visit all of the concessions and find the magic that existed in each one of them before I continued on my journey of discovery.

Dr. Mayo's Mantra

Nothing is what it appears to be, ever.

Don't take it personally, even if it's meant to be.

Every challenge brings an opportunity. (a gift).

The secret is to focus on the opportunity...
*   Not on the challenge.*

Expect nothing,
*   and you will never be disappointed.*

The only thing between you, and your dreams,
*   is you.*

Give yourself permission to fail... So you can
*   give yourself permission to succeed.*

Treat yourself the way you want others
*   to treat you.*

Learn to say 'Thank You,' and mean it.

Forgive others...
*   So you can forgive yourself.*

Art of Magic

Last week the Source asked me to walk with him. As we ambled along together talking, the background slowly transformed itself into that of the Sonoran Desert where I live. We stopped in front of an arched sign fifteen or twenty feet wide supported by two fifteen-foot posts that appeared to be made from a discarded old telephone pole cut in half with one end of each half partially buried in the ground. The large block letters on the wooden sign spelled out 'The Art of Magic'. This sign appeared to be situated in the middle of nowhere with the desert continuing uninterrupted on the other side of it. However, when we passed under the sign, the other side instantly became a bustling carnival with booths running parallel along each side of the wide, central walkway. The Source turned to me and said, "You must visit each of the booths in the 'Carnival of Magic' before you can continue your journey of discovery". Then, he disappeared.

It looked to me like there were an awful lot of concessions. I had no idea where to begin. So, I started at the very first booth on my right side. Almost from the start I became bogged down in a futile effort to discern what the objective was and how I could possibly ever muddle my way through this first booth strewn with all sorts of entrapments. I backed out of there and moved down the walkway to get some idea how many booths there actually were. The pathway was long, so I began 'super walking' with my feet positioned a foot or so above the ground. My actual speed multiplied by two then by four until I was moving rapidly down the column of concessions. When I reached the other end I turned around and continued rapidly back down along the opposite side of the walkway. There turned out to be one hundred and seven concessions in the 'Carnival of Magic'. That seemed like an awful lot for me to muddle my way through.

I stopped a passerby and asked him where I needed to go, which concession was the one that I should visit first. He told me, "Concession number seventy-seven". As it turned out the booths were numbered alternately with the odd numbers being on the left side and the even numbers on the right side. I made my way directly to concession number seventy-seven. It was located on my left side about three quarters of the way down the walkway.

This concession was very plain. There was a long table aligned with the walkway itself. It was draped with heavy cloth touching the floor. On the other side there was a small chest with a large bowl sitting on top. Inside the bowl was a pitcher. Off to one side there was a dressing screen and partially covered behind the screen there was a bed. It was larger than a single bed and smaller than a double bed. Sitting in a chair right behind the long table was a young girl. She appeared to be of Asian heritage, with long, black hair. She was quite attractive, actually. I really wasn't sure what the point of this concession was until she invited me into the concession and motioned for me to get on top of the bed.

Then, I observed this whole scene using my 'Wizard's Powers of Observation'. The attractive young lady was actually a skeleton. She was death, my death. Just to the left and behind the bowl on top of the small chest there was a small metal cylinder about two and a half inches tall and three quarters of an inch in diameter. It glowed faintly. That is what I needed to get my hands on. That is why I needed to come to this concession first. I stopped time, sniped the glowing cylinder and made off with it, held between my teeth, while I vaulted over the security fence running behind the concessions. My death was kept at bay, in a state of suspended animation, as I made my escape.

When my feet touched the ground on the other side of the fence, I found myself in a deciduous forest, lush and green. In the distance I saw a huge tree. Not just huge but ten or twenty times larger than any of the other trees in the forest. That was obviously where I needed to go.

When I reached the base of the giant tree, I had no idea how I might climb it. The first branch was at least eight or nine feet above the ground. I closed my eyes and I began to float upwards. When I reached that first branch, I came to rest on top of it. There was a small door in the side of the trunk of that gigantic tree. It had no hinges, no doorknob and no place to put a key. I pushed the glowing metal cylinder up against the middle of the door and it swung open, as if by magic. Inside there was a huge room, much larger than the diameter of the tree itself. The trunk of the tree was more than twenty feet in diameter, while the room where I was standing was more like eighty by a hundred and sixty feet. At the far end of the room there was a single desk where a very small humanoid was seated in a black, leather chair with a very tall back. I made my way over to where the humanoid was seated. It appeared to me as though it was not actually real but a mannequin or some kind of illusion. With my wizard's powers of observation, I could see beyond the back of the chair where a tall thin man was seated on the opposite side of this two-sided chair. I made my way around to the back of the chair and presented the metal cylinder to the tall thin person sitting there. He immediately stood up and introduced himself to me as "Teacher".

He said, " I see you have found the key to the "Art of Magic". He then asked me to extend my hands out, palms up. He placed his hands on top of mine and said, "I now bestow upon you the 'Gift of Magic'. I thanked him. Then, I asked how I was supposed to use this gift of magic. He told me, "You must learn how to use 'The Gift of Magic' all on your own.

Faith

A couple of nights later I traveled to what I refer to as the Island of Vishnu. I sat down in front of the fire pit, lit a fire magically and waited. The first god to arrive was the Goddess Janaki, consort to the God

Rama, then Shiva the God of destruction, then Hanuman the monkey God, then Ganesh the elephant God, then Krishna and finally a young boy about ten years of age. I had no idea who he was.

When each of the Gods arrived, I asked them if they knew how to use magic. None of them had any idea. The last God to arrive was Krishna. He asked me to put out my hands with the palms up. Krishna then said, "I give you the gift of Faith". He then presented the young boy to me. Krishna said, "This young boy is 'Innocence'. He will accompany you as you pass through the 'Carnival of Magic.' With the gift of Faith, and in the company of 'Innocence', you will complete your journey through the 'Carnival of Magic' safely."

Hot Rocks

Armed with the gift of 'Faith' in the company of 'Innocence' we returned to the 'Carnival of Magic' to acquire the necessary knowledge to be able to use the 'Gift of Magic' and to make the impossible become a reality.

I lifted 'Innocence' over the security fence behind the concession where I had recently escaped from my death. He took the small metal cylinder back to the same place where I had stolen it and unceremoniously presented it to the young Asian woman. She was very surprised to see a child in this carnival where children were never allowed and shocked that he had the magical cylinder, the key to the world of magic, in his possession.

She hugged him, thanked him and joyously carried him to her bed behind the dressing screen. She deftly removed his shoes and socks, retrieved two smooth river-rocks from her heated supply, oiled his feet with virgin palm oil from the pitcher in the bowl on the top of the small chest and methodically messaged his feet with the smooth river-rocks.

After vaulting over the fence myself, I silently made my way further into the concession and witnessed what just transpired with the warmed river-rocks and the palm oil. When the young lady noticed me standing there in the shadows, she came to me, took me by the hand and led me to her bed. She removed my shoes and socks as well as my shirt and placed me face down on her bed. Then I too received her hot-rocks and palm oil treatment. It was truly a magical experience, the magic of touch, the magic of heat, the magic of warm palm oil, the magic of "Hot Rocks" in concession number seventy-seven, Don't miss it if you ever have the chance.

At Bay

Where do we go next? We walked across the walkway from concession number seventy-seven, over to concession number seventy-six. It was completely open except for a narrow gate and a gatekeeper who was dressed like the Ringmaster from a Ringling

Brothers, Barnum and Bailey Circus. He had a tall black hat, a long waxed mustache, a red and black coat with long tails and a black bullwhip that he proudly cracked at will. There was a tall fence surrounding the entire concession. It was quite impressive, all made of steel rods. Inside there was a large Bengal Tiger. I asked the Ringmaster what the point of this concession was. Without hesitation, he informed me that the objective of this challenge was to go into the arena and keep the hungry tiger at bay for four minutes.

When I asked the Ringmaster what happened if you were unsuccessful. He said, "Why you will be the tiger's dinner." As I entered the enclosure I saw a cellophane wrapper on the ground. I picked it up and moved towards one corner. The tiger eyed me immediately and moved towards me drooling from the corners of his wide-open mouth. I crumpled the cellophane several times creating a crackling noise. The tiger hesitated.

Four minutes can be a very long time while waiting to become a tiger's dinner. I threw handfuls of dirt, not at the tiger but up into the air. The fine dust settled slowly, the tiger hesitated. I summoned the smell of a forest fire. The tiger was confused. I created the illusion of a forest fire with crackling sound, with dust for smoke and the smell of burning forest. The tiger's fear of fire subdued his hunger pangs. He retreated into the safety of the far corner seeking his escape. Four minutes were up. Time had elapsed. The ringmaster presented me with a single red rose, the crown of victory.

The gate was opened and Innocence entered. I

presented the single red rose, the trophy for victory, to him. He proceeded immediately over to the tiger and patted him on the head then climbed upon his back. They came together to greet me. Nose to nose, I looked deep into the eye of the tiger. There I saw the forest of his birthplace. I transported him into that very forest where as a young tiger he lived free. I transported him deep into the past, long before men ever came there. I saw him running free in the forest with a red rose in his mouth. He looked back at me just once, before everything disappeared. We were once again standing alone in the Sonoran desert.

Waterloo

Innocence and I were walking with the Source last night. I asked a question about the 'Carnival of Magic'. He said I needed to continue to visit all of the remaining concession booths that were there. I asked him what happened to the concession 'At Bay'. He said, "The tiger is gone. That concession no longer exists." He left us at the gate to the 'Carnival of Magic'. I chose the first booth on the left side, concession number one.

It was completely open. It was a giant field of mud. At its small gate stood Napoleon, the Napoleon Bonaparte, short, dressed in white, with gray-blue winter, wool-coat and tall, black leather Jack-boots. He was holding his funny boat-hat in one hand and a black, leather, riding-crop in the other. I asked him what the challenge was at this concession. He pointed at the sign on the fence. It read 'Waterloo' in bright red letters. His only comment, "Everyone has their Waterloo."

I entered, not knowing what to expect. The mud looked impassible. It certainly was Napoleon's undoing. Once bogged down in that mess, you could never get out. So I chose to 'High Step' with my feet about eighteen inches above the mud and to 'Speed Walk', first doubling and then re-doubling again and again my rate of passage. Around and around I raced covering every inch of that muddy arena until I spiraled into its very center. A black, leather swivel chair appeared on a flat rock in the middle of the sea of mud. I sat down in it and turned slowly in a complete circle facing each of the cardinal directions and as I did so I broke the spell of Waterloo and section by section the entire arena transformed into a lush green pasture surrounded by flowering trees. Everything vanished. Innocence and I were standing alone once again in the Sonoran Desert. I had broken the grip of Waterloo on Napoleon. He was set free.

Shell Game

The Source wanted me to return again to the 'Carnival of Magic'. He told me to go to concession twenty-six. So, we went.

The concession was very plain. There was a small table for two with a pretty young girl seated on the other side. She had three walnut shells in front of her on the table. She was wearing a low-cut blouse with puffy sleeves...very low cut. Her hair was long, brown and curly. Behind her, to my left, was a large security person, of sorts. He looked like a guard straight from 'Aladdin and the Magic Carpet', with his short, fat, curved-sword stuck in his yellow sash, his green, silk bloomer-pants, his pointy-toed slippers and his tiny red vest, three sizes too small, topped off with a twisted purple turban and arms held firmly across his chest. Otherwise, nothing was there, not even a fence.

I sat down on the empty chair across from the pretty little girl and asked what the point of this concession was. She lifted up one of the walnut shells revealing a shiny steel ball bearing the size of a pea. If you can guess where the 'pea' is, you win. If you don't, then you loose. I of course wanted to know what prize I would win and what happened if I didn't win. She said that if I guessed where the 'pea' was, I would win a turtle shell but if I didn't guess where the 'pea' was then I would loose a toe. At that moment a large turtle shell appeared on the ground next to her. I told her that I had no use for a turtle shell. Out of the turtle shell popped a head and four legs. It was actually a live turtle. I had no use for a live turtle as well. I suggested that instead of a turtle perhaps I could have one of the guard's toes. The staunch guard quickly dropped his arms and moved back away. Obviously he was only there to chop off my toes and not to wager his own toes. Then I suggested that the pretty young girl offer her own toes against my toes. She reluctantly agreed. Before we began she added the caveat; once the wager began, it would not end until each and every finger and each and every toe had been wagered, lost or won, meaning we would play this shell game twenty times. The Source had insisted that I visit each and every concession in turn and learn the magic there in. So began the shell games.

The pretty young girl moved her tiny hands swiftly round and round the tabletop, my eyes glued to hers. They were sky-blue, intriguing yet sad. She stopped, waited and winked.

Using my wizard's powers of observation, I discerned that the steel ball was not under any of the three walnut shells. It was held tightly, clinched in her right hand. I grabbed her hand, squeezed it until it popped open, releasing the captive 'pea'.

Again we played the game. This time the steel ball was in her left hand. We played again. The small steel ball was on the floor by her right foot. I summoned it up into my left hand and presented it to her on my open palm. Again she tried. This time I presented the cold steel ball on my right hand. A final time she tried. The steel ball was nowhere to be found. She had made it disappear. I in turn re-created the shiny steel ball from thin-air, picked up the middle walnut shell revealing the steel bearing and placed it into her hand.

Turning to the guard, I said, " I'll take these five fingers from this hand right now"! Everything vanished. I was standing by myself, alone in the Sonoran Desert where I live.

The Source appeared with Innocence. I asked him what the meaning was, of the shell game. He said, "It was a parody, a play on life. When you enter the game of life, you cannot leave until it is over. It is not fair. You do not make the rules. You have played life not to lose. You should always play to win."

Seven Chickens

The Source took Innocence and me back to the entrance to the 'Carnival of Magic' to continue our quest to visit each concession and garner its magic.

I have admitted many times that on several occasions I have been very slow to get what is being presented. I don't consider myself to be that dense but I often struggle grasping concepts that eventually do prove to have merit. We entered the carnival and went to the second concession on the left side, which would make it number three, because all of the concessions were numbered alternately with those on the left-side being odd numbers and the ones on the right-side being designated as even numbers.

This concession was completely open. There was nothing in it but sand, surrounded by a flimsy chicken-wire fence. Inside there was a small funny looking character with big ears and a bald head wearing what looked like a brown home-spun friars, Franciscan's habit. He motioned for us to enter. I suggested to Innocence that he wait outside until I checked the place out. When I entered through the small, rickety-gate, several chickens jumped up and scrambled about. I wasn't sure where they came from. I ended up going back to this concession at least four times before I had any idea what the point of the concession actually was.

I asked the friar, what the deal was with the chickens. He told me they were magical creatures. That I found hard to believe.

I asked the Source about the chickens being magical creatures. This is what he said, " You don't normally think of dogs as being magical creatures but they have been intimately connected to the rise of mankind from foraging primates into formidable predators. That would have never happened without the help of the dog. On the other hand, man's very survival depends on the magic of bees and the magic of chickens, which are the primary providers of food for all of mankind. No creatures are more important, more necessary for your well being than these three, the dog, the bee and the chicken."

The last time we visited concession number three, Innocence entered right along with me. While I was talking with the friar, who turned out to actually be an elf, Innocence sat down in the middle of the sand lot. The chickens all ran over to him. They surround him, sat on his lap, perched on his head and shoulders. I asked the friar what the deal was with the chickens. They had scattered when I came in but they couldn't be close enough to the young boy.The elf said, "Chickens are magical creatures. The boy is a magical creature.

He is Hindu. He is vegetarian. He worships animals. They know that he won't eat them. These chickens here represent the seven original archetypes from which all existing varieties have arisen."

Guitars

I was talking with the Source last night while at the recharging station replenishing and topping off my energy supplies. As time has past, I seem to be burning through greater and greater amounts of energy. He insisted that we continue our journey through the 'Carnival of Magic' and finish before returning to other projects. He advised me that we should go to concession twenty-seven next, when I asked if we should proceed numerically in order down the row of concessions. He added, "If you proceeded in strict numerical order, you would probably be dead already." With his advice we proceeded to concession twenty-seven.

It was right across from where number twenty-six had been, where we played the shell game, but it was gone now. This concession was 'U'-Shaped with a back and two sides. The front was completely open. Guitars were everywhere. They even formed a ceiling of sorts, hanging down on straps and slings suspended in mid-air as though there were an invisible ceiling supporting them. Guitars were on all the walls and standing together in groups supporting each other. There were only acoustic guitars, not any electric guitars. There were the small and large, the bass and the classical, every size, every color and every make you could imagine.

As we made our way through the maze of Guitars, a tall, thin young man approached. He was wearing black pants, a white shirt with an open collar and a black vest. His hair was dark and a bit unruly. He asked if we would like to try out any of the instruments for fit. That sounded a bit odd to me but I'm not a guitarist. I don't know their lingo.

Innocence was delighted with the invitation. He picked up a rather small oddly festooned guitar and strummed his fingertips across the strings. The most beautiful melody I have ever heard flowed out of that small instrument. I had no idea such a young boy could possibly be so talented. The attendant asked me next, if I would like to find a fit.

That sounded even more bizarre to me. I don't have any idea how to play a guitar. He encouraged me to look around and see if anything caught my eye. There was one guitar that I thought was really beautiful. It was smooth and round and polished. The grain was so exotic, the strings psychedelic. When I touched it, I smiled. I strummed it gently. This quiet, wistful sound flowed smoothly out and filled my thoughts with memories of times past, of happiness, of joy and bliss. The attendant said, "It's a perfect fit. It's magic. It's yours." Innocence and I both left with our magical instruments, both were a perfect fit and most of all, free of any charge.

Chimera

Instead of heading off in a random direction, I asked the Source what concession might be the best choice for us to visit next. Without hesitating he said, "Concession seventeen". So, that is where Innocence and I ventured to next.

Concession seventeen was completely open with only one single tree standing alone in its center. Nothing else and no one was anywhere to be seen. If you walked to the back of the concession and looked down the hill there was a good size lake down at the bottom. In the middle of the Sonoran Desert a body of water the size of an acre is a good size lake. If you stepped outside of the un-fenced boundary of the concession, the lake disappeared. As soon as you re-entered the concession's space, the lake returned.

I looked around everywhere but there was nothing but this strange tree in the middle of the concession.

I went over and sat down under the tree and leaned my back against its trunk. Small translucent flakes began to fall down all around me. They were shaped like crescent moons the size of a quarter. They felt like snowflakes but disappeared as soon as they touched anything. When I stood up the flakes ceased their falling. I walked around under the branches of the tree but nothing happened.

The trunk of the tree was substantial. It was between two and a half and three feet in diameter at its base. I have never seen a tree that looked anything like this tree. The tree itself was forty or fifty feet high. The branches of the upper third of the tree sloped downward and the leaves were needle-shaped like a pine tree. The branches in the middle third of the tree grew more or less straight out horizontally. They branched repeatedly and had large deciduous leaves like a maple tree. Branches on the bottom third of the tree pointed upward at a sharp angle and were straight like bamboo with long slender leaves. The bark on its trunk was very old, thick, convoluted and rough to the touch. I rapped it with my knuckles. It sounded hollow.

From inside the tree, a voice was heard, "Knock, Knock, whose there?" I didn't know what to say. I rapped the trunk again.

The voice again said, "Knock, Knock, whose there?"

I was taken aback. I said my name meekly, "Michael".

The voice of the tree responded with, "Michael who?"

I answered, "Michael the traveler". There was only silence. I knocked on the tree-trunk again.

The tree asked, "Knock, Knock, whose there?"

I answered, " Michael the Sorcerer".

Then the tree pulled itself up out of the ground by its roots, took off running, leaving a gaping hole in the ground where it had been firmly planted and quickly replanted itself down by the lake.

I went over to the hole in the ground that was left behind and called down, "Hello. Is there anyone there?"

A voice answered, " Who is there?"

I answered, " Michael the novice Magician."

A ladder instantly appeared and the voice said,

"Come on down." The space was Spartan but it was complete, even to the smallest detail. Crescent moons adorned everything. He was a magician. His name was Chimera the magician. He was the tree.

It was the strangest thing I have ever seen.

White Goat

When I asked the Source where we should go next he said, "Concession five". This concession had a series of U-shaped cordons from its entrance on the left side all the way to the back, similar to what you would see at security checkpoints at airports. This convoluted pathway went back and forth six or seven times. It was intended to facilitate movement of visitors at this concession. At the back of this concession, located on an elevated platform, sat a Hindu deity. He had six heads.

When I exited the cordoned pathway the area cleared and began filling with devoted worshipers of this Hindu deity. There were only adults. There were no children. Everyone was dressed in fine silken attire. The background color of every garment was earthen red. Each of these garments was decorated with various geometric patterns all of earthen-tones. The garments all had long sleeves with snug cuffs at the wrist and ankle. There were no dresses, only pants or pantaloons with long shirts or blouses. Every garment had a short cuff-like collar. Men's collars completely encircled their neck. Women's collars had a narrow opening in front. There were no buttons in front, so they must have been pullovers or buttoned in back. No one wore any jewelry. There were no beards on the men. There were no turbans. Everyone had long hair twisted rope-like into a beehive-bun on top of their heads. Nobody wore shoes. Everyone wore silk slippers with pointed toes that matched the rest of their clothing. Everyone filed into the open space where cordons had been. They knelt down in rows behind small stool-like things.

These small triangular stools were about a foot high. The triangular tops had curved corners. They appeared to be covered with a soft leather drawn tight from underneath. Each stool had three legs, slightly splayed and attached to what appeared to be a bentwood base slightly larger than the tops. These things were extremely light and very strong. They were not used for sitting but used to support your chest as you leaned forward on your knees in prostration before the deity with your forehead touching the floor. When the room was filled with devotees I looked up from where I was kneeling. The deity was no longer there. In his place was this magnificent white, longhair goat. The goat paraded back and forth on the low platform then proceeded over to where I was kneeling, bent down and kissed my forehead. He went back to the stage, walked around some more, then returned to where I was kneeling and kissed my forehead again. He did this three times. This whole scenario left me with many questions in my mind. So, the next night we returned to concession number-five.

Naigamesha is one of the forms that Kartikeya takes. He is the god of war and is depicted with the head of a goat.

This six-headed God was Kartikeya, brother of Ganesha and second son of Shiva and Parvati. He carries a spear in one hand and blesses worshipers with his other hand. His six heads stand for his six virtues and allows him to see in every direction to see danger coming and to fend off the six demonic vices: Kaama (sex); Krodha (anger); Lobha (greed); Moha (passion); Mada (ego); Matsarya (jealousy).

I asked Kartikeya several questions about the attire of his devotees and the small stools: Why no jewelry; why no beards; why no turbans; why no skin showing except for the hands and the face; why no head coverings; why no adornments; why no shoes; why no bare feet; why no dresses; why only red and earth tone colors; why no chanting; why no bells or gongs?

Katartikeya said that out of devotion to him and his six virtues and respect for each other they follow a conservative religious protocol intended to ward off the six demonic vices.

I introduced the child, Innocence, to the God Kartikeya and told him that he was the embodiment of innocence, sent by Krishna. Kartikeya said, "The greatest virtue of all is Transcendence, innocence is its very heart."

I asked Kartikeya what the three goat kisses were

for. He said that they were his gifts to me of the three virtues: The gift of Wisdom, the gift of Courage and the gift of Temperance.

Volition

When I asked which concession we should visit next, the Source said concession number seven. This concession had a stone-wall all the way across its front built out of solid blocks of granite that were about sixteen inches square. In the middle of the wall there was an arched entrance way. There was no door, no gate and no gatekeeper.

Just inside its entrance way there was a very attractive young girl. She invited us to come inside. There was absolutely nothing inside except a hard-packed dry-dirt surface to walk on. The sides and back were fenced in. Before I could even ask what the objective of this concession was, we were frozen in place by some kind of force. Neither Innocence nor I were able to move in any way. There was a hot-pink beam of light coming across the front and back of the concession space and a green beam of light, which crossed both ends. These light beams must have been the source of energy that immobilized us.

I didn't take it personally and I didn't become angry. I mobilized and concentrated my 'Intent' and my 'Will'. From the right side of the concession space a flame-front quickly advanced, un-creating the green and pink energy beams and their creators. In a flash and a bang there was a great explosion and Innocence and I and the young lady were thrown out into the surrounding desert. The concession and its granite walls were vaporized. The 'Carnival of Magic' was gone. Now, there were just the three of us alone in the Sonoran Desert. One question for me now was, "What do we do with this girl?"

That makes a total of eight concessions that we have visited so far and during that process four of them no longer exist.

G. I.

The next concession the Source wanted us to visit was number thirty-seven. In front there was a single table with one young man dressed in military attire sitting behind the table. There was a long line of people winding slowly towards that table. Each person would fill out a bunch of papers and then proceed to the 'starting point' where they would dress down to their underwear and carry their stack of papers along with them through a series of stations. The first thing they did was to separate us. I don't know what happened to Innocence and the young girl. As for me, they made me wait and wait and wait. Then they isolated me, insulted me, interrogated me, intimidated me, asked me all sorts of dumb questions and subjected me to physical and mental abuse. So, I left and retrieved Innocence and the young girl, then took them to a safe place. I returned to concession number thirty-seven two more times before I understood what the magic was that resided there in that concession.

The third time I returned, I approached the concession from high above and descended slowly straight down upon it. That is when I discovered the point of the concession. That is when I learned its magic. They used their magic to turn innocent young people into soldiers trained to follow orders, trained to kill upon command, trained to disregard civility and respect for others, trained to destroy any and all obstacles in their path. It was the magic of 'robotic thought', the magic of 'robotic action', to kill or, to be killed, to show no mercy and to take no prisoners.

I too was a soldier. I too was trained to kill. I was trained to destroy. I practiced every day, for four years of my life, to destroy all creatures that lived on the face of the earth, to make it, our one and only home, uninhabitable. Now I am tasked with saving it from the Galactic Council, which has sworn to destroy all of Humanity.

Black Sheep

I asked the Source last night where I should go next. He said that I wasn't ready to go to concession number two yet or to the last concession, number one hundred and seven. He thought I should visit number nine since

I had already been through one, three, five and seven. That will make five concessions in a row on the left side at the 'Carnival of Magic.' He didn't add that I have also been to seventeen, twenty-seven, thirty-seven and seventy-seven on the left side but to only two on the right side, which were twenty-six and seventy-six. Both of them no longer exist.

Concession number nine was completely void of anything. It was barren dirt enclosed by a fence. As I stood there looking around, a long metal tube about twenty inches in diameter appeared. Out of it shot one small black sheep after another until there were nine, baby, black, sheep huddled together in the middle of this deserted space. Where was the magic here? I couldn't even tell these nine black sheep apart. They all looked exactly the same to me. So I stopped time and then reversed it. When I again resumed time, I marked each of the sheep as they popped out of the metal tube with a white number right on the top of their head. I placed a rope collar on each of the black sheep. Then I tied a reed onto each collar and strung the young sheep together with reeds into a little caravan of sheep from one to nine. Number one was the most energetic and curious and nine was the most docile and lethargic. Around and around they went in ever widening circles until they covered the surface of every inch of dirt within the concession.

With their passing they enriched the soil and green grasses began to grow until the dry packed dirt inside of this concession was transformed into a verdant green pasture.

The magic of black sheep is that they can turn a wasteland into great farming country just with their passing's.

Makeup

I asked the Source where I should go next and if I should take Innocence or the girl along with me. He told me to go to concession seventy-one and to take both of them along with me. So, we wrapped our two arms around each other with the girl standing on my left side and Innocence standing on my right side just as though we were going to play a game of Red Rover, Red Rover.

When we arrived at concession seventy-one, we were greeted by three young ladies each with their own personal makeup-stool with its short, cushioned back that we then sat down on. The stools were surprisingly comfortable, each covered in a different pastel-color of soft suede. I was seated on the left side. The young girl was seated in the middle and Innocence was seated on the right side. We were separated from each other by almost eight feet. Behind us was a long wall of cabinets with a narrow countertop separating the storage cabinets below from the glass covered shelves above that were lined with all sorts of bottles and vials, brushes and other sundry makeup stuff including wigs, beards and even mustaches. I didn't know what the point of this encounter could be or what kind of magic this place might possess.

The makeup lady, who was with me, appeared to be Native American. She was very attractive but her eyelashes were extremely long, obviously fake. She began with my hair. She was working very close to me. When she began working on my face I looked deep into her dark eyes and was pulled into a car sitting next to her. I was in the driver's seat and she was the passenger. We were stopped on a hill at a stop sign. We were in the middle of the desert. There was a small house down at the bottom of the hill to my left on the driver's side of the car. We got out of the car and walked down to the house. There I met her brother Nathan. I accompanied Nathan on several adventures while his sister completed my makeover.

When she finished her work, I appeared to be a totally different person. I had long straggly gray hair hanging out from under this strange-looking floppy, gray-wool hat. My beard was long and gray. I wore a floor-length shabby gray hooded robe. My shoes were crudely made of rough stitched leather. I had a tall wood staff in my right hand, a long leather sash with a leather pouch attached to it around my neck and over one shoulder. Both of my hands and my face were smudged with dirt and soot. I told her what I had seen and experienced while staring into her dark eyes. Her brother must be a spirit-walker and a shape-shifter. While I was with him I helped to rescue several different spirit animals. I asked her what I was supposed to be and what the magic of this concession actually was.

She said, "The magic in this place makes you up, dressed in your original form. That is 'who' you were. At heart, that is 'who' you really are. You were and are and always will be a Druid. What you 'saw' is 'what' you really are. You are a seer. You are a shape- shifter. You are a spirit walker and always a Druid."

I looked over at the young girl. She was made up as Cleopatra. That must be who she really was. I asked her what her name was. She said everyone calls here Maria but her real name is Maritza. She looked like Cleopatra to me. She was beautiful.

Innocent was dressed up as a cabin boy from a sailing ship from the eighteenth century. I asked him 'who' he was. He remained silent. Perhaps some things are better left unsaid, better left unknown.

The Dungeon

I asked the Source where we should go next. He said we should go to concession number thirty-four. When the three of us arrived at concession thirty-four there was nothing there but a thick stone wall with no doors or windows and no way to get through it.

Yet somehow we ended up on the other side of the wall. From there, two heavily-armed guards brandishing spears, wearing metal breast-plates and helmets with short swords dangling from the waist bands of their armored metal skirts, dragged us down marble steps into the dungeon below. It was cold and dark and damp. We transported out of there together as fast as I could open a portal. I took Innocence and Maritza back to the safe place where they had been before and left them there. I needed to return to concession thirty-four by myself and seek out the magic that dwelled in this strange place.

Thick stonewalls encircled this concession. The central arena was just powdery, dry, dirt. Stone stairs led down to the dungeons below. These two guards were Roman soldiers. This place obviously was a Roman prison. I ventured back into the dank, dark dungeon seeking its magic powers. There I remained, bathed in solitude and silence for a long time knowing that nothing is actually ever what it appears to be.

I returned to Maritza and Innocence. She looked beautiful dressed as Cleopatra. I asked her if she were real or just an illusion. She asked me what I wanted her to be, real or an illusion. I told her I Just wanted to know for sure if she were real or not.

I held her hand and asked her, "How can I tell if you are real or just an illusion."

She said, "Hold me close and kiss me."

I held her close, kissed her and she was gone.

I finally concluded that the magic within those four stonewalls did not a prison make but prison in reality is found within the dungeon of our minds.

Yester-year

The next concession in the Carnival of Magic the Source wanted us to visit was number twenty-three. Where we arrived was very familiar. It was in the middle of the Sonoran Desert exactly where the Carnival of Magic was normally located but nothing was there but desert. We looked all over the place. There was nothing there but desert. While we waited for something to happen, I fell asleep. When I awoke, Innocence was nowhere to be seen. While looking for him I found a small white business card. The card had a name on it and the word Yester-year. The name on the card was Colin Roberts. I thought his business card might help us un-ravel the mystery of what had happened to the carnival and where concession twenty-three was.

We went to the closest information center. That is sort of like a library where information is exchanged and stored. While we were at the information desk seeking information about Colin Roberts, a delivery person brought in a bundle of supplies for the center. The lady at the information desk said, "That is Colin Roberts".

I asked Colin if he knew anything about where concession twenty-three was. He told me it was part and parcel of the Carnival of Magic. He volunteered to take us there, where he was actually its manager. On our way he added that this concession was owned by the business of 'Yester-year.' Its specialty was 'yestering' I had no idea what yestering was. He said that everything about concession twenty-three was yester... Nothing was today. Everything was yesterday. It didn't even exist today. It never exists today. It only exists yesterday.

When we arrived at the concession it seemed very much like a carnival booth. It had a duck-shoot, a baseball throw, a basketball hoop, a dartboard and loads of overstuffed animals hung from ribbons that were prizes players might possibly win. Colin was just another typical carny. He invited me to try my hand at the baseball throw. I stepped up to the counter to get my baseballs. Colin handed me a bowl of boiled red potatoes, coated with olive oil, parsley flakes and black pepper. He said they were freshly made but they were all stone cold. Then again, everything here was 'yesterday'.

Three Seals & a Lion

The Source said that at this point, there were any one of several concessions that we could go to. I asked about number eleven. He said we were ready for that one, so that is where we went.

When we arrived, I was surprised there were no people anywhere. The whole concession was a giant water-filled arena with an oval island right in the middle. Sitting on the island were three seals. Once we arrived, the three seals started their well-choreographed performances. They did all kinds of crazy stunts and intricate maneuvers. After each of their many pieces were complete they would all fly out of the water landing on the oval island, bow, clap their flippers together repeatedly and bark loudly at each other. Their performances were marvelous to behold. After the show ended and was complete a giant sea lion appeared, from I don't know where, with a large bucket of raw fish and began flipping them to the three seals on the island with his teeth while the seals barked and clapped their flippers.

We made our way over to where the sea lion and the three seals was seated and congratulated them for such a magnificent performance. I asked them what the magic was here in concession eleven.

They looked at each other puzzled and replied, " We all speak English."

Palmero

I asked the Source last night if concession nineteen was O.K. for us to visit next. He said that he thought we would be able to navigate our way through concession nineteen successfully.

Many of these concessions are very strange. It is always a challenge to find the magic within them.

Surrounding this concession was a large, split-rail fence. It was about seven feet high. The rails and vertical posts were made of solid, hand-hewn logs about nine-inches square. There was about nine or ten feet between the vertical posts. Inside the arena there was soft dirt where many large animals had obviously been kept. I looked down to see the clothes I was wearing. I had a heavy leather glove on my left hand but nothing on my right hand. My pants were blue, Levi-denims. My shirt was a western cut worn under an old faded leather vest. I had a red bandana around my neck, cowboy boots on my feet and a tall western hat on my head. Innocence was similarly dressed. It looked like a place for riding broncos.

As we walked across the enclosure to the far side, I was suddenly looking down into a frying pan with a little cooking oil inside. Divots of ham, which looked more like prosciutto, were falling down into the frying pan followed by divots of white onion then divots of green bell-pepper. The divots were all similar in size and shape. They must have been cut out with a small circular hoop-knife. The divots were about three-eighths of an inch wide and three-quarters of an inch long. After these were sautéed together, small green olives were added. Anisette was added at the very end to finish the dish. This was served over long-grain white rice, accompanied by a glass of Anisette. This dish was traditionally served prior to the competition of the 'riding of the bull' held every Palm Sunday in Segovia Spain. It was the year of our Lord, Eighteen Seventy-six. The dish was called 'Palmero'.

There was a huge bull in the shoot. It had a single rope around its chest and back. That is what you hold onto when you 'ride the bull.' I lowered myself onto the back of the bull. Innocence was lowered down right behind me.

The shoot opened. The bull walked slowly out to the center of the ring, kneeled down and bowed his head low so Innocence and I could get off easily. We were declared the winners of the prize of Segovia's 'Palmero' riding of the bull, for the coming year. The prize was a filigreed nine-inch wrought metal cross.

I accepted the cross graciously and asked what the magic in 'Palmero' was. I was told that the cross of 'Palmero' had powerful magic. It could cure the sick and do many other marvelous things.

I immediately took it to a friend who was not feeling well, placed it on their head, their back, their chest, their stomach and their legs and summoned the powers within the magic filigreed cross of 'Palermo', to make the sick well once again.

'Palmero' in Spanish refers to men who work with palm trees.

Cave-Rock

Last night I asked the Source if it was all right for us to visit concession number twenty-one. He said it should be O. K. for us to visit that concession. We went straight away to concession twenty-one. When we arrived, there were seven black-hawks flying single file in close formation right over us heading somewhere. This concession was a rookery for black-hawks. There were twenty more hawks waiting in line to join the other seven. That made a total of twenty-seven black-hawks in a hurry to get some place. I shape-shifted into a hawk myself, an especially large one and very black at that, then I followed them to their destination.

We were in Navajo country, dry, desolate, with little vegetation. We swooped down towards a large flat rock and passed under the exposed edge on the east side of the rock, right into a cave. Immediately I knew exactly where we were. This was the 'Cave of the East'. These creatures were 'spirit hawks'. They were shape-shifting Navajo Medicine Men. They paid little attention to me. I watched intently as they prepared themselves for the ritual of entry into the spirit-world of the Navajo, through the sacred 'Cave of the East' whose whereabouts is known only to Medicine Men of the Navajo Nation. I followed behind them as they entered in silence and secrecy, single file, into the 'Spirit World of the Navajo'. I was anxious to discover the magic that lay hidden within the confines of this cave.

To a spelunker this cave would be called an alcove not a cavern, for here there were no tunnels, except the tunneling within their minds. Each of the medicine men held a bundle of coiled luminescent threads in their left hand. With their right hands they strung the glowing threads creating a pathway and forming a tunnel like an orb-spider spins its web. Out of the emptiness and darkness a luminescent, glowing cave emerged. I followed, as what was familiar descended into the unknown, the spirit world of the Navajo. This luminescent tunnel opened into the eternity of the Navajo past, where their memories re-united with the remembered. The plants, the animals, the people, the places, all became reality. They all became rememberings.

Navajo medicine men use these rememberings to re-connect to the past and use the power within that past to alter the present, just as a wizard uses the power of their imaginings to alter the present by connecting it to the future. A Magician likewise uses the magic residing within everything to accomplish almost anything, while the shaman will dive deeply beneath the surface of the earth to gather their knowledge, wisdom and energy from Earth Mother.

Therein lies the importance of our history. Therein lies the value of historians, the validity of oral tradition and tribal rituals.

The medicine man blows smoke or spittle onto the sick or dying person attempting to re-connect their wellness of the past to the un-wellness of the present through their rememberings blown out with the healer's breath.

Only by remembering what we actually were, can we know who we truly are.

Magic Mike

Last night Innocence and I visited concession number twenty-three. The Source told me it would be O.K. for us to go there next. This concession was much more like the kind of carnival I grew up with. Out in front of the concession was a midget standing on an elevated booth shouting as loudly as he could, "Magic… Mike…the…Midget. Over here… Come here.

Take a chance…Win a prize" The prizes were lined up all in a row, ten very colorful children's books. They were all different, one for each of the numbers, one through ten. The game was a classic coin toss.

Toss a coin into a glass bottle …Win a prize, not just any bottles but different size milk bottles for different size coins. There were ten small antique glass cream bottles for pennies numbered from one to ten, five half-pint bottles for nickels, four quart bottles for quarters, two half-gallon jugs for fifty- cent pieces, and a one-gallon jug for silver dollars.

I felt right at home in spite of the fact I didn't have a single coin in my pocket. I knew right away where the magic resided in this concession. There is powerful magic in those ten numbers, in those ten symbols, if you know your math. They created the world we live in, our world of technology, machines and prosperity. They created everything we have everything we do, everything we are.

Odds of winning anything with the toss of a coin, here in this concession, were very poor.

Samsara

Last night I asked the Source if it would be O.K. for me to go back to concession number two, the first one on the right side as you entered the 'Carnival of Magic'. That was where I initially started but obviously wasn't prepared for what I encountered. The Source said that I might be able to successfully manage it by now but I should definitely not take Innocence with me to that concession.

I wanted to be prepared for whatever I might run into so I took everything with me that I have accumulated from my many adventures. Instead of trying to open the door, I kicked it in. The door slammed shut behind me. It was completely dark. Small glowing eyes appeared around me. With my ability to see in complete darkness, which I acquired in Hades, I made my way down a narrow pathway. It ended in a 'T' with a path going to the right at ninety degrees and a path turning left also at ninety degrees but no way to go forward.

I projected my awareness as far as I could to the left and then to the right. The path to the left ran through barren desert and sand dunes with zero vegetation. The path to the right passed through a turbulent stormy ocean: Two very poor choices…

I took both paths at the same time. I fast-walked both with my feet almost two feet above the surface of the sand and water. They both eventually ended at different locations on the beach of the 'Sea of Uncertainty, which separates the 'Sands of Time' from the 'Event Horizon'

I looked to the left and I could see myself several hundred yards away standing on the beach looking out upon the 'Event Horizon'. I looked to my right and I could see myself far down the beach to the right looking out on the 'Event Horizon'. I had traveled both pathways successfully and found my way to the 'Sea of Uncertainty'. There was a disturbance far out on the event horizon. I moved towards it from both my locations simultaneously. We arrived together on a small sandy island, united and again we were one. When I turned around I was met by Samsara. I had four arms and quickly overpowered Samsara and dismembered him with my sword and my magic.

We returned to the beach-sands of time where we started. One of us stayed behind with Samsara who had magically re-assembled himself, for the Gods are indestructible. I returned to concession number two, opened the door from the inside and escaped. But I was transformed in the process. I left behind the desire for things. I no longer wanted things. I no longer needed things. I understood the nature and power of attachments. I understood the reality of impermanence. I had vanquished Samsara but at a great personal cost... My ignorance. For everyone knows, "Ignorance is bliss."

Ice-Rink

The next night I asked the Source about concession number twenty-nine. He said that would be fine but I should take Innocence along with me, for sure. When we arrived, I was totally surprised. The only thing there was an ice-skating rink like one used for ice hockey. Right in the middle of the desert there was this full-sized ice rink. Innocence had never seen an ice rink before. I had no idea where the magic resided in an ice rink. Was it like, "A Miracle on Ice"? We went back several times over the period of a few days trying to figure out what the magic was in the ice rink. Last night Innocence and I returned for the fifth time. We finally sat down on the ice and had a long in-depth conversation about what the ice rink was and where the magic in it might reside.

Was it like the 'chicken and the egg', which came first, water or ice? Two hydrogen atoms plus one oxygen atom make water. Two hydrogen atoms and two oxygen atoms make hydrogen peroxide, a rocket fuel. That seemed like the wrong track to me for us to be on.

What if it weren't ice? Maybe it was an illusion. What if it weren't water but some other kind of ice, like dry ice, (frozen carbon di-oxide) or maybe frozen methane or frozen something else? The surface was solid, smooth and very white, maybe too white. Maybe it was a fourth form of water or the frozen form of white light.

When we were standing outside of the rink it was located as the twenty-ninth concession in the carnival of magic. As soon as we stepped onto the surface of the ice, everything outside of the rink disappeared. There was only desert. The rest of the carnival was gone. When you stepped off of the ice, the carnival was back. This phenomenon gave me an idea.

What would happen if I were in two places at once, on the ice and off the ice at the same time? But, I was concerned that I might loose Innocence in the process, so I had him stand in front of me so I could hold onto him while we stood right next to the edge of the ice rink. We stepped outside of the rink together with one foot and left the other foot inside the rink on the ice. When we moved our heads outside of the border of the rink, there was nothing, absolutely nothing. It was total blackness, total emptiness, totally void of any thing. When we put our heads back inside the border of the rink, the desert returned but there was still no carnival of magic outside.

If we stood outside the rink, there was what appeared to be an ice rink in the midst of a carnival.

If we were inside the rink on the ice the carnival outside disappeared and what we saw was the virgin desert. If we were in both places at once the rink existed alone in the midst of the void, the place of emptiness or some similar location.

The ice was smooth. It was hard. It was cold. It was white but maybe too white. This had to be something other than frozen water. In the desert you see mirages all the time shimmering in the heat of summer. They look like water but they are not water. They are illusions. What we were standing on was not a mirage. It was time – frozen time – an ice-rink composed of time frozen solid. Nothing exists outside of time. Time animates all things. Where there is no time, nothing exists. Everything is only a memory.

We looked up and there was a Zamboni. It was smoothing the surface of the ice. As it moved around the rink, the ice disappeared with its passing. The oval-shaped edge remained. We moved inward as the Zamboni spiraled in tighter and tighter circles around the rink until nothing remained but the oval-shaped edge of the rink, the rink of frozen time. The Source was driving the Zamboni. The Zamboni and its driver disappeared.

It was all an illusion. In the end, time itself was nothing but an illusion. We are awareness, nothing more... animated by time, which itself is only an illusion, a mirage shimmering, alone in the desert.

Monkey Business

Last night I asked the Source if it would be O.K. for us to go to concession number thirty-one next. He thought it would be all right for us to go there now. Innocence and I were surprised when we got there by the tall tongue & groove fence surrounding this concession. It was about eight or nine feet high with no windows and only a single gate or door if you could call it that. The gate was cut out of the fence with a round arched top. It had no doorknob and no handle. The gate or door if you prefer was made out of the same 1 X 6 tongue & groove siding you would find on a house, just like the rest of the fence was made from. The fence was attached to 4 X 4 red wood posts. The fence like the door was only one board in thickness. There was a small window cut into the door no bigger than a 3 X 5 card with a clear glass pane located right at eye level.

Sitting astride the top of the fence with one leg inside and one leg outside the concession, was a chimpanzee or female lowland gorilla. It was hopping on its rear end along the top of the fence towards us making loud gorilla grunts. I looked into the concession through the tiny viewing window. Inside there were all sorts of slides and swings, children's games and a merry go-round. There was a carousel with all sorts of different animal figures that children could ride on.

A big black male gorilla's face suddenly filled the viewing window. It was absolutely huge and very menacing, so I decided we would pass on this concession for now and come again another day.

This concession turned out to be operated by gorillas. All of these contraptions were for children to play on. I can't imagine what kind of monkey business goes on inside, let alone what kind of magic might be in there.

A couple of nights later we went back to concession number thirty-one to see what we could discover about this concession. We went very early for us, just after midnight. This time we approached the concession from directly above. Down below we saw several adult human maintenance staff hustling around. They were cleaning up and attending to all of the gorillas and other animals as well as a lot of children. None of them were real. They were all robots. They looked real. They sounded real, moved around autonomously like they were real but they were actually real-looking robots like "West World".

The magic in this place was actually 'Illusion'. The objective was "Suspension of Disbelief" a very powerful combination.

Big-Top

I asked the Source if there were any other concessions that I shouldn't go to at this point in the process. He said that I could go to most any of them now. Some of them might still be problematic for Innocence to visit but he said he would advise me in advance if that were the case. I thought about going to number thirty-three that is right next to thirty-one and just across the central walkway from thirty-four, both of which we already visited but in the end I decided to go to the very last concession, number one-hundred and seven.

Innocence and I approached this concession from high above. We drifted down slowly so as not to be easily seen. It looked to me like a giant red and white umbrella with its alternating red and white segments, like the spokes on a bicycle wheel. As we got closer and closer it became obvious that this was not an umbrella at all but the elaborately decorated top of a giant tent with its single mast-like center post. This was a gigantic tent. It reminded me of the big-top circus tents from the bygone Barnum and Baily traveling circus days.

When I was a kid, the whole town would turn out at the train station to welcome the once a year occasion of the circus coming to our town. The kids got out of school. The adults played hooky from work or claimed some unknown illness. No one wanted to miss the huffing and puffing big, black steam engine pulling the circus train into town or the elephant parade down main-street. Fifty-cents would get you a seat for the 'greatest show on earth'.

Even the sides of this giant circular tent were corrugated with alternating red and white stripes. Innocence and I crept cautiously into a side entrance hoping no one would notice us. It was the craziest thing I have ever seen. There were hundreds if not thousands of people milling around but no one was talking. It was ominously quiet. There were no children and no women, only old men wearing long floor-length robes, all drab, all faded, all spun from heavy wool. They all sported long gray beards, wore pointy hats bedecked with stars and moons, ambled aimlessly around like lost kittens. It was as though we were invisible.

Starting at the outermost part of the circular arena, rectangular columns started popping up, one for each of the multitude of magicians. One by one each magician was lofted up on top of a column as it rose up to its pre-determined height. This process continued around and around the arena with each succeeding revolution being a foot or so shorter than the preceding one until finally the entire arena was transformed into an amphitheater. As this process unfolded we were forced further and further into the center of the arena. By the time this process ended we were stuck right in the middle in a small circle not more than ten feet in diameter with a single old man toting a walking staff. He addressed me by my first name. Then, he presented me with a soft, long robe of silver-gray wool and a small glass jigger-size cup. Everyone rose to their feet and clapped loudly for me in adulation. They assumed I had completed the task of visiting every concession in the 'Carnival of Magic' but I had not.

It seemed obvious to me that the magic within this concession was not in the concession itself but resided squarely within its occupants.

Garlic-Toss

Next we went to concession number thirty-three. There wasn't much there. Two bare-chested young men were running this concession, which was comprised of only two attractions. One was a take-off of the familiar beanbag toss. The other was the typical sledgehammer/ bell ringer ploy. Both of them were rigged so they were impossible for you to win.

My focus remained on the hidden magic in each and every concession. The two young men seemed enamored with each other so, they had no magic. The two games were familiar and simple, so probably no magic there. While trying to divine the hidden magic, my mind wandered back to the long wool robe and the dinky little glass jigger given to me by the ancient old magician. I retrieved the jigger from my coat pocket and examined it closely. It was quite odd yet seemed somehow familiar. I finally realized that this object was actually an eyecup, which in the past was used to hold medicaments to wash out your eye.

I put the eyecup up to my eye and peered through it. Everything was distorted. When I looked at the pile of garlic heads used in the tossing game, they glowed with hidden energy of some kind. That must be where the magic resided, there in the heads of garlic. From there I returned to concession number one hundred and seven. There was nothing there but an upside down red and white umbrella. When I looked at it through the eyecup, the gigantic big-top tent re-appeared. The magic was in the umbrella and magic was in the garlic, both revealed by the ancient glass eyecup.

Burlesque

Last night I ventured to concession number four, the second concession on the right as you enter the 'Carnival of Magic'. There was an elevated platform about twenty-four feet wide and three or four feet above the ground. It was maybe ten feet in depth. It had no ceiling and no back but there was a 4 X 8 ft. piece of plywood on both sides. Across the very front of the plywood sides at the top there was a round rod supported on either end that held the 'stage' curtain, which rolled up and down between performances. The stairs to get onto and off of the stage must have been at the back.

Nine young women came out in single file and formed a straight line. They were wearing black short-shorts, a gold garter around their left thigh and a gold colored loose fitting silk blouse. On their feet they were wearing black, laced, tap-shoes. They began dancing in unison swinging their arms like tap-dancers always do. When they finished their tap dancing, the curtain came down.

When the curtain went back up the dancers' shoes and blouses were gone. The dances were more sensual. It was like the Folies Bergere. The curtain went down ending that part of the show. The curtain went up again and the dances and dancers were very provocative, wearing nothing. When the curtain fell, out from behind the curtain on the right side bolted a demon, giant, ugly, menacing. He towered over carnival goers, sniffing the tops of their heads. Some he passed over, some he snorted on and they vanished to some unknown torture and unseen death. He sniffed me and passed on over to Innocence. There he sniffed Innocence once then, it disintegrated and fell onto the ground in a thousand shards, fizzled and vanished.

The magic here was not in the concession nor in the dancers nor in the dances but in Innocence. Innocence itself is very powerful magic and also very powerful medicine.

Puppy Dogs

Innocence and I went to concession six next. It was encircled with a short wire fence less than two feet high. It was one of those garden fences that have extensions on the ends of each two-foot section that you push into the ground for support. Each section was linked to the next section by two loops that hold the sections all together. There were no gates anywhere. In front of the concession there was a young girl in her late teens. She was wearing tan riding pants, high black boots and a riding helmet. It was a complete riding outfit. Her hair was done up in two tight pigtails. She was the only one there. She was the keeper of the concession.

The whole elliptical enclosure was full of ten- week old puppy-dogs. They were everywhere. They all looked like Golden Retrievers. The young girl invited us in. When Innocence walked in the puppies were all over him. When I stepped in I only got a few feeble sniffs then they were off for the guest of honor, Innocence. I guess there is nothing quite like a young boy with a bunch of puppy-dogs. There was no question in my mind where the magic lay in this concession.

Dogs are very special. But puppies are truly magical creatures.

8 & 10

First we visited concession number eight, then we visited concession number ten. There was a problem with concession number eight. It wasn't there. Instead of a concession there was a giant hole in the ground, a bottomless pit. I had no idea what kind of magic could create this hole in the ground and I had no idea where I should look for the hidden magic there in so I decided to move on to the next concession, number ten and try our luck there.

Concession number ten was a giant concrete slab with a painted red line starting at the outer edge and spiraling in towards a single pipe sticking up out of the center of the slab. It looked to me like a spiral maze with the end being in the center. I put Innocence up on my shoulders and we started to follow the red line as it spiraled inward towards the central pipe.

As soon as I stepped onto the cement slab everything turned into a dense jungle. The painted red line was covered with dead leaves. The spiral path we were going to follow was impossible to see. Not only was the jungle foliage thick it was also tall. There was no way for me to navigate towards the central pipe, which was now buried and overgrown. I took one step and a wooden set of steps blocked our path. It was three steps high. I climbed the three steps with Innocence still on my back. When I stepped off of the third step everything turned into a complete desert of nothing but towering sand dunes.

I had no idea where we were or what we were supposed to do. I was completely baffled by both concession number ten and number eight. I turned around and backtracked as quickly as I could.

When we were once again outside of the cement slab, Innocence got down from my shoulders and was standing next to me. I wanted to get his perspective on these two concessions so I asked him to tell me what he saw. His response blew my train of thought completely.

Innocence said that he saw pristine desert at both concessions. He didn't see a giant hole in the ground at concession number eight and he didn't see anything but desert at concession number ten. The question for me to answer now was how could he see nothing but normal desert in both places when what I saw was so bizarre?

We returned to concession eight. I put a blindfold over my eyes and walked out into the open-pit. Nothing happened. I was still standing on solid ground. This must be an illusion, an illusion for me but not an illusion for Innocence. We went back to concession ten. I did the same thing there. I put the blindfold over my eyes and walked out onto the cement slab. There was no slab. There was no jungle and there were no wooden steps and no sand dunes beyond. There was only the pristine desert that Innocence described.

If concession eight was an illusion for me, how should I describe what concession ten was. It must be more than an illusion. It must be delusion. I was delusional. What could create this illusion for me? What could create my delusions? They could have only been created by real magic. That was the magic in concession number eight, the power of illusion. In concession ten it must have been the power of delusion. That is truly powerful magic.

What is the difference between the two? Illusion comes from the outside like a mirage in the desert heat of summer. Delusion comes from within one's own mind, from one's own personal memories as your brain attempts to interpret an illusion and give it a reality of its own creation.

Innocence was insulated from illusion by his mind that was open and accepting to all new experiences. He was insulated from delusion by his mind that was unfettered by my mind's multitudes of memories competing with reality.

Desert Ducks

Last night we went to concession number twelve. When we arrived at concession twelve, there were no people. There was an oval-shaped berm about three or four feet high with desert all around it. There were more trees around the berm than you would normally see in the middle of the desert. On the other side of the berm there was a lake. It was a big lake to be found out in the middle of the dry desert. My estimate would be about sixty by ninety feet and probably with water only about eight or nine feet deep.

When Innocence and I came over the crest of the berm a mother duck and her ten ducklings scurried out of the reeds at the edge of the lake and swam single file out to the middle. Close behind the baby ducks came the father. He was a beautiful teal-headed Mallard.

It was amazing to witness this family of water birds peacefully swimming together in the middle of the hot dry desert. That was truly magical. Nature itself is pure magic there for us all to see. It's up to each of us, to open our eyes. It is up to each of us to see and appreciate the magic that nature surrounds us with.

Guns & Roses

Innocence and I went to the next concession on the right side of the carnival of magic. It was number fourteen. It was really exciting, almost like an Old West show with horses and cowboys, six-shooters and marksmen. There was one cowgirl there with her lever-action 44-caliber rifle that was really the star of the show. She looked like Annie Oakley. She was shooting from horseback, shooting standing, prone and backwards, using a mirror and even blindfolded. In one trick-shot, she shot the stem of a rose held in a cowboy's hand, then picked it up and put it between her teeth. The whole show was very entertaining but I had no idea where the magic might reside in this concession. I asked the cowgirl if she were 'Annie Oakley'. She said that she was the embodiment of all things 'Annie Oakley', not

Annie Oakley herself.

She told me that, " Real power comes from the barrel of a gun". Then she said, " Having a gun can protect you and your family from the 'Tyranny of Government' and the feel of a gun is real magic. It makes me the equal of any man". She gave me her red rose and told me it was her magic. I put it between my teeth and Innocence and I departed.

Earth Mother

The next concession that Innocence and I visited was number fifteen. It was just across the way from fourteen. This place was nothing but pristine desert in its natural state. While we were standing there wondering where the concession was and what it might actually be, a rift began to encircle the entire space.

The whole thing rose up into the air. It had to weigh thousands of tons. There was nothing visible that was supporting it, a giant scallop of earth larger than a tennis court, floating there, leaving this crater at least fifteen or twenty feet deep. The edges sloped down from a few inches to at least fifteen feet or more in the middle. I left Innocence above standing a safe distance from the edge as I ventured deep down into the pit.

Sitting in the center of the bottom floating a foot or so off of the ground was a man dressed in a white robe. He was in a deep state of meditation. He barely looked up when I approached. I asked him what was going on. He told me 'Earth Mother' created us to care for the earth and all the plants and animals that live here. Earth is the perfect place for us to live. No place in the universe is more perfect. I asked him, "Where was the magic that resided in this concession." He said it is everywhere you look. It is in the soil, the air, the water, the plants, the animals, yes even in us with all our shortcomings. We too are magical creatures. We just don't know it.

Clowning

Last night Innocence and I went to check out concession number twenty. The only thing there was a very tall clown with a bunch of large balloons floating in the air tied to strings tethered to his waist-belt. I looked all around but saw nothing else.

His shoes were way too big. His nose was way too red and round. His hair was way too yellow and straw-like. His fingers were way too long. His voice was way too deep. His eyes were way too beady.

To engage this strange clown in conversation, I commented, "Helium balloons"? He said, "No." I asked what kind of balloons they were. They looked to me like extra large helium balloons tugging on their strings.

He said they were magic.

I asked how much.

The clown said a dollar.

I reached into my pockets but found no money in

any of them, held up two fingers and said, "Two."

He untied two balloons, a red one and a green one and gave them to me. I tied one to Innocence's wrist and the other one around my wrist, reached into my pocket and found two dollars that were not there moments before. I handed the two dollars to him. He folded them up and put them into his pocket, then handed me a five-dollar bill and said, "Change." He was way too strange.

At that moment a doorway appeared, no door, just a doorway. It was about four feet wide and twelve feet tall. Innocence and I walked through the doorway. On the other side we floated away, carried by our two magic balloons. We floated over a city that reminded me of the streets in Disneyland. We descended slowly and landed safely in the middle of Piccadilly Square in Old London Towne.

Carnie

Last night Innocence and I visited concession number fifty. There really wasn't anything there except for a small, elevated wooden platform with a true 'carnie' standing on it yelling as loud as he could, "Over here, over here! Come this way! Get it now! Win it! You can do it! Anyone can do it! You can be a winner! Today's your lucky day."

There was nothing else around. There was no one but this wild Carnie plying his trade of selling you a bill of goods. I was focused on trying to figure out what and where the magic in this concession could possibly be. Maybe it was the art of the sale. Maybe it was in his hyper-activity. Maybe it was the innate gullibility that exists in each of us. 'A sucker is born every day,' or so they say.

As I intensely focused my attention on this carnie character, a strong wind of some kind began to blow. First it blew away his hat, then his clothes, then his flesh, leaving only a skeleton yammering away, still trying to hustle any and all within ear-shot. Magic must ultimately lie in the mind, not of the deceiver but within the mind of the deceived. The carnie was capturing your attention with his display and spiriting it away, convincing the unwary that they really could win something at his rigged table in his crooked lair.

Perseverance

Last night Innocence and I moved on to concession number one hundred and six. It was located directly across the central walkway on the right side from the very last concession of the 'Carnival of Magic'. The only thing there was an old lady who was sitting in an antiquated wooden rocking chair knitting something while she rocked slowly back and forth. Her rocking chair sat on top of a section of wood flooring about seven by seven feet square. There wasn't anything else around.

I struck up a conversation with the old lady.

She seemed somehow to be out of place there in the 'Carnival of Magic'. I had no idea where 'magic' might reside in a scenario such as this. I introduced Innocence and myself. The old lady congratulated me on having visited all of the concessions in the 'Carnival of Magic'. I had actually only visited about a third of the concessions so far but I left it at that.

When I asked her who she was she said, "Perseverance". I said, "Your name is perseverance?"

"No", she replied. "My name is not perseverance, I am perseverance." I asked her about the magic in concession one hundred and six. She told me that there was magic in perseverance. She said that she was perseverance and she was magic. She then handed me what she had been knitting and said that it was magic.

The thing was beige in color and made of some kind of soft wool-like stuff. It was about the size of a handkerchief. It felt very soft, fuzzy and warm to the touch. I asked what it was. The old lady said it was like a 'Thneed', it was a sock, a shirt, a pillow or pants, a hat, a glove or bag. It was magic. It could be anything or do anything you asked it to do.

Stock Yard

This concession was number one hundred and five. It was surrounded with eight-inch wood posts buried four feet apart. They were almost seven-feet high and had five separate strands of twisted fencing wire, like barbwire minus the barbs, strung along them. The lowest wire was less than a foot off of the ground. The highest wire was about six and a half feet above ground level. The other three wires were evenly spaced between the top and bottom wires. Each wire was threaded through a separate hole drilled through the center of each post. Somebody went through a lot of trouble to put up this stockyard fence. The front of the concession was almost a hundred feet long. There were no gates anywhere. On the inside the soil was dry, dusty and obviously had been trampled by an awful lot of animals.

I left Innocence outside the enclosure while I investigated. After squeezing between the wire fencing I walked around inside the enclosure. It was only about thirty feet or so from front to back. There were no animals anywhere so I helped Innocence to come inside with me.

No sooner had he set foot inside the enclosure than it was teeming with cows and goats, deer and buffalo, sheep, antelope and other ungulates. The back of the enclosure expanded exponentially off towards the horizon. I hustled Innocence through the fencing and back outside. As soon as he was outside, all of the animals disappeared and the back of the enclosure returned to its former dimension of about thirty feet.

While I was attempting to leave the enclosure and squeeze back out between the fence wires, Innocence gave me a hand. As soon as his hand touched mine, the animals all returned. He was obviously a part of the magic here in this Stock Yard.

I knew right away that the only place we could discover where the magic originated and how it worked was from there inside the stockyard. So Innocence came back inside the enclosure and we went in search of someone who could explain what was happening.

Far away near the back of the enclosure, I could barely make out someone sitting in a chair of some sort. We made our way through the herds of animals to where the person was sitting. It took us awhile to get there because it was pretty far away and all the herding animals didn't help with the process.

When we finally got there I asked the man, who turned out to be a Native American dressed in buckskin attire, what was going on. He informed me that all of the animals were spirit animals. They trusted Innocence because he, like all of them, was innocent by his very nature. I on the other hand was guilty of all sorts of infractions. Magic by its very nature exists in the state of innocence and in the minds of the innocent.

Three Tortoises

Innocence and I made our way over to the next concession, number one hundred and four. It was right across the way from the Stock Yard. This concession had a short fence around it. The fence was about twenty inches tall and was made from what looked like old wood lath, the kind of lath used to plaster walls. The vertical pieces of lath were unpainted and about half an inch apart. The fence itself appeared to be very old but the desert both inside of it and outside of it appeared to be completely undisturbed as though this rectangular fence with rounded corners had just been dropped there from out of nowhere. There were no gates, no people and nothing inside the fence except desert.

I stepped over the fence and three desert tortoises appeared in the center of the fenced area. When Innocence stepped over the fence the three tortoises disappeared. When he stepped back out of the fenced in area the three tortoises re-appeared. I walked out to where the three tortoises stood staring at us and squatted down to get a closer look at the three tortoises, each turned into an Indian shape-shifter. In the midst of us four, a small fire-pit appeared complete with its burning fire. The first shape-shifting Indian on the left side took out what we would probably think of as a peace pipe. He puffed on it until a large cloud of smoke circled above his head. This cloud of smoke took on the shape of a coyote. He passed the pipe to the second shape-shifting Indian who puffed on the pipe until he too produced a large cloud of smoke. It morphed into the shape of a bear. The smoke-bear swallowed the coyote. The pipe was then passed to the third shape-shifter. He too puffed and puffed until there was a large cloud of smoke above his head. It morphed into an Indian chief complete with a full headdress of many feathers. Then he passed the pipe to me.

I puffed on the pipe several times until I too had

created a large cloud of smoke. It hovered over my head for a short time then turned into an ancient Druid. I asked the shape-shifting Indian Chief where the magic resided in this concession. Was it in the shape-shifters or in the tortoises or perhaps in the magic pipe. He said, that for Indians, smoke was magic. It always revealed the true nature of things.

The smoke-coyote revealed the true nature of the shape-shifting Indian. He was really a coyote masquerading as an Indian medicine man. Likewise the smoke-bear was actually a bear masquerading as a shape-shifting Indian. I was truly a Druid Priest masquerading as a shape-shifting time-traveler. He on the other hand was in reality a magnificent Indian Chief in the guise of a medicine man, both servants to their tribe.

The smoke slowly dissipated and I was once again eye-to-eye with three desert tortoises each with one red eye, one sky blue.

Buffalo-Bear

Innocence and I visited concession number one hundred and three next. For me it was reminiscent of a rodeo arena with one exception, the wooden structures were massive compared to the ones I have seen in other places. These wood members were dark brown and steeped in creosote. They formed a rectangular arena with rounded corners. The height of these massive containment fences was at least nine feet, maybe even more. At the far end on the left side there were five chutes lined up in a row next to each other. There were no people anywhere. There were no gates into or out of the chutes. Nor were there any entrances into or out of the arena itself. The space between these vertical wood posts comprising the containment fences was about ten inches. That was the same size as the square wood posts that formed the fences. I couldn't squeeze through the openings between the posts and I couldn't reach the top of the fences to climb up on them. We waited around for over an hour for someone or something to show up but nothing was happening. With Innocence' help, I was finally able to get up on top of the chute walls. From that vantage point I was able to clearly see the entire layout.

On the inside of the arena, right in front of the chutes a familiar figure appeared. He was the young Indian that I have encountered on other adventures in the past. He was bare-chested, wearing only leather jerkin pants and moccasins. He had a red headband with a single feather dangling from his dark, braided hair. He motioned for me to jump down into the first chute. I shook my head and motioned for him to jump down into the chute. When he did so he turned into a giant buffalo with his own face. After he popped back up out of the chute he once again motioned for me to jump down into the chute. I did so and transformed into a white buffalo with my own face. We moved on to the second chute.

The young Indian leaped into the second chute and he became a giant Grizzly bear. After he popped back up out of the second chute, I jumped down into it and transformed into a white polar bear. From there we moved on to the middle chute, number three. I motioned for him to jump in but he just shook his head and waggled his index finger from side to side so I jumped into the third chute. I fell a very long ways into complete darkness. When I finally landed I recognized the place immediately. I was in Hades. Because I acquired the skill of seeing in complete darkness when I was in Hades in the past, I was able to escape unscathed and popped up out of chute number three.

The young Indian refused to jump into the fourth chute so I jumped into it and ended up where the river Styx enters the underworld. I returned unscathed and asked the young Indian what was in the last chute. He told me 'Death' so I passed on that last chute. Then I asked him what was in the arena. The young Indian smiled and said, "Tomorrow", then disappeared leaving me to wonder about the magic in this concession or does the magic lie in tomorrow.

Time Mirage

Last night, Innocence and I visited concession number one hundred and two. It was unusual. It was simply an oval-shaped smooth surface with no borders. There was virgin desert surrounding this shiny smooth surface, no fence, no entrance, no exit and no people. It was like a mirage in the desert but it wasn't shimmering and it wasn't even hot there in the desert. Innocence thought it was a smooth flat surface of water reflecting the sky from its glass-like surface. I thought it looked more like a giant mirror of some kind, larger than a tennis court.

Innocence put his finger in, then his hand and then his arm up past his elbow. When he pulled it back out it was gone... completely gone but the feeling was still there. After a few moments his arm, then his hand and last of all his fingers re-materialized.

I had Innocence remain outside of the concession to monitor what transpired. That is when I stepped out onto its shiny surface and everything went black.

The face of a young lady appeared before me. She and her surroundings completely filled my field of vision. As we talked she told me she was my son's girl friend. She was blond. Not bleach-bottle blond, just blond with light brown roots bleached by the sun. I asked her several questions. She volunteered some information without me even asking.

She said that she and my son have not yet met. She said she was twenty-seven years old and her name was Sally. I think her last name was Struthers.

She lived in Portland Oregon. My son lives in Orange County. She teaches sixth grade. She is divorced and has one daughter who is seven years old. Her daughter's name is Malissa with an "A". Her daughter was born in April. My son has a daughter who is also seven years old. She was born in September. Her name is Michaela. That would make them about seven or eight months apart in age. Sally said that she and my son will not meet for eight or nine more years. I was gone for almost an hour. When I stepped back off of the shiny smooth surface, back into my own time and place. I too arrived and then re-materialized. I sensed my body as being whole even though it had not yet materialized completely for several more moments. There seems to be a relationship between how long you are gone and the rate at which you completely re-materialize. It was sort of like awakening from a dream. Obviously I had stepped into a 'time mirage' that was located in the middle of the desert, smack in the middle of the 'Carnival of Magic'.

As we turned to walk away, a small character appeared. I asked who he was. He said that he was the Caretaker of the 'Time Mirage'. I asked where the magic was in this concession. The Caretaker said, "Magic resides only in the mind of the observer".

Stockade

Last night Innocence and I visited concession number one hundred and one. It was located between 103 and 99, right across from 102. As we approached the concession there was nothing there but desert. Suddenly a stockade appeared. It occupied the entire space between 103 and 99. Each concession is about seventy-five feet deep and fifty feet wide. Some concessions are a bit larger, some are a bit smaller but the size of this concession was about average.

The stockade itself was constructed from rail- road ties, steeped in creosote, brown, sticky and stinky. The vertical ties had one end buried in dirt. They were erected six to eight inches apart with horizontal railroad ties attached to the tops. The inside was lined with fencing made from eight-gauge steel wire with four-inch square openings. It looked like something you would use to reinforce concrete. The wire also extended across the entire top supported by steel cables stretched tight from front to back. These cables were about eight feet apart and were woven through the squares in the steel wire fencing to support it.

There were no people anywhere. There was no way to get into or out of this fortified enclosure. Inside there was a single animal running around like crazy, a Tasmanian Devil. We waited there a long time before we left. No one ever came. We went back on three different occasions but there was never anyone there. I couldn't figure out where or what the magic was in this concession. The most peculiar thing about it was that it disappeared when you left and re-appeared when you got close enough to it. You had to be closer than twelve feet for it to materialize.

The first time we went I had Innocence stand back more than fifteen feet. I put a blindfold over my eyes and proceeded to walk into the enclosure. With my vision completely blocked the concession never rematerialized. I sat down in the middle of the desert where the concession should have been and began to meditate on where the magic resided in this concession.

A tall thin Indian appeared and sat down in front of me with his legs crossed. He was shirtless, wore leather pants and deerskin moccasins and had a red headband with a single feather sticking up in back. It wasn't an eagle feather. I don't know what kind of feather it was. I wasn't familiar with a feather like that. He asked me what my name was. I told him and then I asked him what his name was. He asked, "What's in a name?" I asked where the magic was in this concession.

He said, "Magic is illusion. You need three things to create illusion. You need a specific time, therefore timing is essential. You need to have perception therefore your vision is necessary. You need a place. Your name is a place, an address in time and space. I asked if he were a shape-shifter or if he was that crazy Tasmanian devil.

I asked what kind of feather he wore. He said, "Turkey... a wild turkey feather." Then he laughed.

Bamboo Jungle

Innocence and I visited concession number one hundred late last night. This was an average size concession, about forty or fifty feet wide and seventy or eighty feet deep. Once again there was no one around. There was what looked like bamboo scaffolding about three or four stories high with no building inside. Scaffolding was the concession. We walked all around it before I approached it. I told Innocence to stay away from the scaffolding. I tied his left hand to my right hand with hemp rope. He was told not to enter the scaffolding no matter what happened to me. I grabbed one of the supports of the bamboo scaffolding with my left hand. I was cast instantly into the midst of a bamboo jungle, a forest of dense bamboo towering thirty or forty feet into the sky. My right hand was now completely freed. My left hand was bound to the bamboo with the same rope that had previously bound our hands together. Innocence was nowhere to be seen. I assumed he was safe outside of this strange bamboo concession.

I had no idea how to extricate myself from this bamboo thicket. Bizarre things began to unfold one after another. There was no sense of continuity or connection to my reality. In the final event I was talking on a phone with an Oral Surgeon. I wasn't sure who it was at first. He didn't want to get off of the phone. Finally I recognized his voice. It was John Wenass. He has been dead for over ten years. I told him that I would come to where ever he was over the phone line and take him to where ever he wanted to go. Once I extricated him from where he was he said that he wanted to go to Cabo San Lucas, a resort city on the southern tip of Mexico's Baja California. John told me that he had been in this bamboo jungle ever since he died. This must have been his Purgatory. When we arrived in Cabo, John said that it was perfect, just the way he remembered it was the first time he visited in the fifties. John had several different fishing boats there in Cabo over the many years that he vacationed there in Mexico. He loved it there. This was certainly heaven for him.

When I finally made my way back to concession one hundred, I asked Innocence about how long I had been gone. He said over three hours. It was three hours and twenty minutes by my clock. That was one crazy place. I'll have to return and see if I can find out more about the magic that resides in this concession.

Maybe it's in Cabo. That's what John would say.

Black Hole

Last night Innocence and I went to concession ninety-nine. It was the strangest thing. It was nothing but a giant black hole in the ground. It wasn't just a hole but completely black. There was no way to tell how deep it was. You couldn't get an echo back if you yelled into it. Anything you tossed into it just disappeared. Nothing ever hit bottom. The sides were sheer, straight down and completely black. Light wouldn't penetrate the blackness. Even light disappeared. I have never seen anything like it.

After a while a little man appeared. He was sitting in a fold-up, wooden director's chair. He was almost bald. A few of his straggly, gray whisks of hair were tussled about by the wind. I asked him if he knew anything about the black hole.

He said, " What black hole?"

I pointed at the huge hole in the earth and said, "That one."

The little old man said, " The only hole I see is the hole in your head. That giant black hole exists only within your mind. It is magic, my magic. It is deep magic, powerful magic. Ask your friend there, pointing at Innocence, if he sees a giant black hole in the middle of the desert, in the middle of a carnival, in the Carnival of Magic."

I turned to Innocence for affirmation. He shrugged and said, "I don't see anything but desert."

I turned to the little old man. He and his black hole were both gone. Concession ninety-nine was never anything but plain old desert, never anything more than pure old magic.

Oakley

The next concession we visited was number ninety-eight. The only thing that was there was an old lady sitting in a wheel chair with a lever action rifle across her lap. Another old lady was pushing her around in her wheelchair. There was nothing else but desert, no people, no nothing.

Before long they started shooting the place up.

It turned into a sharp shooting exhibition with the whisky bottle blasted out of the air, the tin can shot off the top of the head, the cigar blasted out of the mouth of the assistant. It was like Annie Oakley resurrected, Annie Oakley to the rescue.

As it turned out they weren't a couple of old ladies in a wheel chair after all but two guys dressed up to look like Annie Oakley, with a replay of the famous sharp shooter's tricks put on display.

When they finally finished their routine and the smoke from the black powder drifted away, I asked the two imposters where the magic was in this concession. After all, that was what I was supposed to discover here in the Carnival of Magic.

They said in unison, "The magic is in the 'Oakley', the magic is in the name. Annie Oakley is pure magic. Annie Oakley gets 'em every time."

Transport

We went to visit concession number ninety-seven late last night. There was absolutely nothing there. When we stepped into the area where concession ninety-seven was supposed to be we were instantly transported into an area of desert where there was no carnival, just empty desert. The only thing there was a tiny sign the size of a 3 X 5 index card attached to a thin stick stuck into the ground that was less than two feet high with the number '97' on it. When I picked it up we were again instantly transported to another place. This place could magically transport you anywhere but I had no idea how to control the magic in this concession.

Heck-tor

Last night Innocence and I visited concession number seven. I had not talked with him for several months. He appeared to be older now. It never occurred to me that a magical character like the 'Embodiment of Innocence' would actually age. He had gained a little weight, grew a little taller and his blond hair was now a little more sandy-colored. His eyes were no longer that piercing, sky-blue but were now a cloudy-gray. He now appeared to be on the other side of ten years.

It always amazes me when I see the 'Carnival of Magic' sign standing alone in the midst of virgin desert landscape with its curved wooden arch high above the ground supported by weathered timber posts, its faded circus letters beckoning to the unwary surrounded on all sides by a sea of silent desert vegetation. As soon as we passed under that sign, the 'Carnival of Magic' instantly appeared as though it had always been there. We made our way down the left side of the central walkway to where the seventh concession was supposed to be. Nothing was there but empty desert and a small rectangular white sign canted off at an angle to one side with the number '7' painted on it. I looked over at Innocence and asked what he thought. He said, "It's beautiful." I didn't see a thing.

He took my hand and we walked into the most fantastic concession I have ever seen. The entire concession space was jammed full of Rube Goldberg creations of all kinds. In the midst of all these contraptions sat a little old man. His long gray hair was frazzled. The top of his head was as bald and smooth as an onion. His colorful vest was two sizes too small. The cuffs of his trousers were rolled up several times. His spindly legs could hardly support his mismatched socks.

As always, my task was to discover the magic hidden within each concession. When I asked the strange little man why I didn't see anything until after Innocence took my hand and we walked into the heart of concession number seven together. He replied, "For every child the world is magic." I then asked the little fellow for his name. He said, "My name is Heck-tor. Grownups cannot see the magic hidden within concession number seven because they just don't give a 'Heck'.

Jimmy 'B'

Innocence and I moved on to concession number thirteen the next night. As we passed by concession number seven I could see everything as though it had always been there, with that strange little man still sitting in his chair smiling at me. He waved at us as we passed by. I guess I finally gave a 'Heck'.

When we arrived at concession number thirteen there was nothing there but an older man who was wearing sunglasses, shorts and a Hawaiian shirt, sitting under a beach umbrella with thirteen red and white panels holding a mixed drink in his hand. The rest was just desert.

I asked the fellow under the umbrella what he was drinking and he said, "What will you have?" I said I would like a Mai Tai and a Shirley Temple for Innocence. The drinks appeared instantly on a small table next to the beach umbrella. I tasted mine. Sure enough it was a Mai Tai, the best I have ever had. One taste and we were at the California beach with the ocean in the distance. Several beautiful girls strolled by, all wearing their bikinis, all of them 'tens'. Innocence didn't even give them a glance. The guy with the Hawaiian shirt looked so familiar. I asked him if he was Jimmy Buffett. He said, "Yes."

I said, "You should be drinking a Margarita in 'Margarita Ville' and we were instantly in 'la playa' by 'del mar' with beautiful 'senoritas' strolling by. I recognized this place. It was Mazatlan, Mexico and I could hear Jimmy Buffett's song playing in my head.

I asked Jimmy where the magic was. He said, "It's all in how you make the Margarita."

Mind Worm

Innocence and I ventured next to concession sixteen. There was no sign indicating it was sixteen but its location was between fourteen and eighteen and directly across from concession fifteen. There was nothing there in that space but desert and a single easy chair with an old lady sitting in it. She wasn't ancient but was older, perhaps in her late fifties. Her gray hair was short and held tightly against her skull. Her unbuttoned, old, blue faded sweater seemed conspicuously out of place in the warm desert. Her intense, unrelenting stare was creepy. She was unresponsive to any inquiries that I made. There was a strange smell around her, somehow familiar to me yet unidentifiable.

We ended up going back to concession sixteen several times before I got a handle on what was unique about it. I tried everything I could think of to get the old woman's attention. I walked over every part of the concession seeking clues or insight. I even touched her hair, her clothing and her chair. Everything looked real enough but it all felt very strange like it was made from Styrofoam or plastic. I finally asked Innocence what he thought. He said that he didn't see anything. That gave me pause. Eventually I discovered a large worm partially buried behind the old woman's chair. It was a worm of some sort, a very big one. It was as big around as my little finger and maybe ten inches long. It had no legs or eyes. It was definitely a worm but not like any worm I have ever encountered.

When I discovered the worm and stooped to pick it up a small non-descript man appeared out of nowhere. The old lady and her easy chair vanished as well as that strange smell. He said, "I see you finally found it." I asked him to explain.

"That worm you found was a 'mind worm'. I used it to create an illusion in your mind, the illusion of an old lady in an easy chair. I created her from your memories. I channeled her chair and clothing through you olfactory nerves. That was what you smelled. The magic in concession sixteen is 'mind worms' and how to use them to create magic in the mind's of others."

Puppies on parade

We went to concession eighteen, last night. It was full of puppies from three to six months of age. They were the perfect age for adoption. There were no purebreds there, only mongrels and mixed breeds. They were there for the taking, just for the asking. They were all rescued from various dog-pounds. That's what they call euthanasia centers for animals.

Nice, Huh?

The puppies all loved Innocence. They ignored me. Adults like purebreds. Children love mongrel puppies. They're all different. They're all unique, one of a kind, just like the children. Puppies are magical, so are children. They drive you crazy but they are still magical. At least they don't chew on your shoes and pee on the carpet.

It didn't take any time to see the magic here. It was everywhere wagging their tails.

Lego Land

Innocence and I went to concession twenty-two next. It was completely filled with Lego things. As we entered the Lego concession all of the Lego stuff became animated. The characters began to move around interacting with each other and the cars and trucks and different machines made their appropriate sounds as they began to move about. The further we proceeded into Lego Land the larger the characters became or the smaller we became. Eventually we made our way to the center of Lego Land, all the way to what I refer to as the 'Lego Guy'. By the time we arrived at the heart of Lego Land every thing and everyone had lost all of the blockish Lego-ness and were very realistic and the same size as us. Lego guy could even talk.

When I asked him what was magical about this place, He said, "Everything. This is how children see Legos. They see them as magical, as real as everything else, because to a child the world and everything in it is magical. You are experiencing Lego Land now, exactly the way a child perceives it, something as an adult that you have completely forgotten how to do.

Gnomes

When Innocence and I arrived at concession number twenty-four, no one was there. It was plain desert with an oval path just inside where the boundaries of the concession were. It was wider than a bicycle path but not as wide as a single lane road would be. The surface was hard and dark and level. We waited around for a while before we left.

Later when we returned there was a central portion of pathway added inside of the oval. It was like an 'X', that crossed in the middle. Each arm of the 'X' had two sides that outlined a paddle shape. There was still no one there so we left and returned again later on.

This time when we returned there were tracks laid on the hard surface of the oval as well as down both sides of the paddle shaped surfaces of the 'X'. The tracks were for a narrow gauge railroad, a very narrow gage set of rails that intersected the oval rails at the four curved sections of the corners of the oval. This was very odd. Still no one was there so we left again and returned a little later.

When we arrived this time there were several very small ore cars dispersed throughout the layout of narrow gauge tracks. They looked like they were made for small children. Once again there was no one there so we left and came back later.

When we arrived this time each car had a Gnome inside of it. The ore cars were racing around the tracks in a frantic chaotic fashion. I don't know what was powering the ore cars. The Gnomes were rocking back and forth and side to side. Apparently that was how they steered them. I don't know how they kept from crashing into each other. At the intersection of each of the arms of the 'X' and the oval tracks there was a dark skin female directing traffic. They were quite small like Pygmies but they were definitely not Gnomes. One of the Gnomes appeared to be in charge. I went up to him and started asking questions. He spoke perfect English. I was thankful for that. I asked a lot of questions. This is what he told me: When I asked about the four Pygmies he referred to them as females, not as women or ladies or girls. He said that females were not allowed into the mines where the Gnomes mined for gold. I asked about them all being very dark. He said white females are not allowed into the gold mines because they bring bad luck.

I thought Dwarfs mined for gold. He corrected me and said that Dwarfs mine for diamonds and precious stones. Gnomes mine for Gold. Dwarfs horde gold and precious stones but they don't mine for gold. I asked where the magic resided here. He gave me a surprised look and said, " We are the magic. Gnomes are magic. You can't even see us unless you, like a child, think in magical terms."

Jerold

Innocence and I went to concession number twenty-eight next. It was completely black. I mean black, black. Everything there including the desert looked like it was covered in black soot. The person standing at the front of the concession, totally covered in black soot, was Jerold Stewart. The last time I remember seeing him, he was seventeen and I was around twelve years old. That was sixty-four years ago. He looked just the same as the last time I saw him. He was a large seventeen year old then, packing a lot of extra pounds and he looks exactly the same now except he is totally black from top to bottom. On Sundays, we had Bible study together before church began. I never was prepared for the discussions. He always was. He always memorized whatever scripture was to be discussed. He knew it by heart, backwards and forwards. I struggled just to read it.

When Innocence and I arrived, Jerold walked up to me, straight away and said, " We came to save your soul from the Devil." Jerold always said he wanted to go to school to become a preacher. I always avoided religion like the plague. Apparently he became a minister. I still try to avoid religious confrontations any way I can. There was a guy sitting behind a piano off to the right and there was a lectern behind Jerold. On the other side of that were several rows of pews and further still there was a wall with a large stained glass window in it. I asked Innocence what he thought of this whole thing. He said that he didn't see a thing.

Apparently there was no magic in religion. Magic emanates from the innocent mind of a child not from religious dogma and intolerance.

Turnstile

Last night Innocence and I went to concession number thirty-two. It looked exactly like the entrance to a subway. There was a single turnstile through which everyone entered. I told Innocence to wait until after I had gone through the turnstile to make sure everything was safe enough for him to follow me. As soon as I stepped through, everything disappeared. Just as soon as I stepped back out everything reappeared. I asked Innocence if he saw what I saw. He said that he did. Then I asked Innocence to step into the concession. Everything again disappeared. It re-appeared when he stepped back out of the concession. So, I assumed that we needed to go through together.

I asked Innocence to get up on my shoulders. As we went through the turnstile a subway train pulled up, stopped and the doors popped open but there were no passengers riding on the train. I had no idea where the train would take us or how we would get back, so we walked back out through the turnstile. The next time we went through the turnstile we passed through the turnstile one at a time like we were supposed to. When we did, the subway was transformed instantly into beautiful countryside with green grass, flowers, magnificent trees and Guernsey cows grazing peacefully on the hillside. Where might magic be in this concession? It could reside in nature or perhaps it could reside in the nature of being honest. Regardless of your current situation, you should never jump a turnstile, trying to avoid paying your fair share.

Farmer John

Last night we went to concession number thirty. When we got there, a farmer was tearing up the desert with his tiny tractor. First he bulldozed all the vegetation away then, he furrowed the sandy soil and drilled it full of crop seeds. After that he sprayed it with liquid fertilizer from a big plastic tank pulled behind his puny tractor. He installed sprinklers, drilled a deep well to supply water for the sprinklers from the underground aquifer and waited for the corn to grow. The crop didn't amount to anything because of the poor soil and burning desert winds. He ended up getting nothing but shriveled up corn- cobs. I witnessed this whole series of events like it was time-lapse photography. Every few seconds another day and another night passed. In the end he pulled up stakes and drove off into the sunset leaving behind demolished desert landscape that could take hundreds if not thousands of years to return to its once prime desert ecosystem. I turned to Innocence and asked if he saw that whole fiasco.

He said, "A giant dust-devil came. It whirled around and around for several minutes before it left. Dust was everywhere. When the dust cleared away the desert was completely unaffected. It was still the same as before."

That was when I understood what the magic was in concession number thirty. The Magic was in the desert ecosystem that allowed for all the many forms of life to flourish in this extreme heat, intense light, sand storms and unbelievable drought.

Thirty-Six

Next Innocence and I went over to concession thirty-six. The entire space of the concession was dark. Inside the concession space was this giant creature. It was black and still smoldering. Its wingspan was fifty or sixty feet. All of the feathers on its body and the parts of the wings close to the body were gone. The flight feathers were all intact and spread ready for it to fly. Its legs were elephant-like. Its head was definitely not that of a bird. It was of that of a monster, a demon or a devil. As we watched, a giant lowboy trailer backed up into the concession space. It was at least thirty or forty feet wide and well over a hundred feet long. It was like something that would be used to move a giant rocket to its launching pad. It was pulled by what looked like a giant airplane tow vehicle. The beast flapped its wings and rose up and landed on the lowboy trailer. The whole thing moved back and away from the concession space and vanished. I had no idea what was going on.

I asked Innocence if he witnessed what I did and he concurred completely. I was intent on finding out what had just transpired. I thought the sign had said thirty-six but upon closer investigation there was a space between the three and the six and in very small print above and to the right of the six was what appeared to be an apostrophe and an 's', such that it read three (3) sixes (6's) which is 666. That is the demonic sign of the Devil.

We returned again to concession thirty-six to

continue our search for the truth into what actually happened there. Pure pristine desert greeted us with no indications that any of the things we saw left any traces. In the center of the concession space there was a small marker with a white X on top of it. As we were examining the space different creatures came up to us and engaged us in conversation. Their communications were clear and precise. Innocence and I were both shocked at this apparent boon in our telepathic capacity. I had never communicated with ants and butterflies, flowers and grass, even gophers and skunks. It was crazy. Each of them had their own story to tell. I was still in the dark about concession number thirty-six.

Later when I engaged the Source and asked him about what happened at concession thirty-six and the number 666. He told me that the small sign did in fact have a three and a six on it but nothing else. There were several black smudges left on it by the smoldering creature that I misinterpreted. He told me that the giant creature was actually a dragon, a magical dragon, the Hell-fire Dragon, which lived inside the cone of an active volcano, the Hell-fire Volcano. From there I went in search of this mysterious Hell-fire Dragon.

When I met the dragon I complemented it on its magnificent size and the incredible volcanic cave in which it lived. During our conversations the dragon told me that the magic within concession thirty-six lay entirely within him and his ability to bestow the powers of telepathy onto all those around him. That is why we were able to communicate telepathically so effectively with all the plants and creatures. Before departing, the Hell-fire Dragon bestowed upon me the gift to communicate telepathically with anything.

Spiral Tower

Innocence and I moved on next to concession number thirty-nine. No one was around. There was a single structure, sitting smack in the middle of the concession space. It was a stone tower at least thirty feet high and more than twenty feet in diameter at its base. It was all white and looked like it was made entirely of limestone, like from the inside of a cave. It had spiral stairs winding around the tower three times that was a little more than two feet wide, more like twenty-six inches. As the stairs spiraled around the structure it became smaller and smaller. At the top the tower was a little more than ten feet in diameter. There was no hand railing. Each step was six or seven inches in height. There were sixty-four steps up to reach the top, which was concave like a shallow bowl and filled with water. At the base of the tower there was a narrow trough with a crude spigot that released water when you jiggled it. The whole structure was made of limestone and filled with water, in the middle of a dry, dry desert. The vegetation and landscape surrounding the tower appeared to be undisturbed as if the tower had some how been dropped from the sky.

I was completely baffled by the whole thing. I wasn't sure who or what I could ask about this strange water tower.

I remembered the gift of telepathy bestowed upon me by the Hell-fire Dragon, so I tried it out on a nearby cactus. There was a Cholla cactus close to the stone tower. I asked it for information about the tower. The Cholla cactus told me that it existed in the past when the weather was fair and it exists in the future when the weather is nice. This was the way that it could survive the extreme environment in which it was physically located. The Cholla cactus told me that its awareness was not in the present and therefore it could not provide me with meaningful information about anything in the present moment. That was weird!

Next I asked the structure itself. The tower told me that it exists in the past and in the future, unlike myself. For me, the past is gone and the future never comes. I am imprisoned within the passing moment, the here and now. The tower told me that it exists in the past, when there were artesian springs providing an endless source of fresh water and in the future when artesian springs would once again be abundant. I was merely experiencing the brief moment between the past and the future. My reality is infinitesimally small while the reality of the Spiral tower' is infinitely long.

I asked the Spiral Tower where the magic was hidden in concession thirty-nine. The tower replied, "Artesian water in the middle of the desert is pure magic".

Feline Phantoms

From concession thirty-nine, Innocence and I moved on to concession number forty. It was on the other side of the Carnival of Magic directly across the central walkway. Once again, no one was there. The concession space was completely filled with young green, rye grass that had never been mowed. It seemed so out of place in the middle of the desert where most plants are gray-green at best. There was a very short wire fence of sorts around it, like something you might put around a flowerbed to keep young people from inadvertently stepping on your flowers. These concessions are so curious. I never know what to make of them.

As we were looking at this grassy field, a young goat appeared in the center of it and was busy eating the new grass. I wasn't sure what to make of it so I asked the kid goat what it was doing. It said that it was eating the grass. I asked why it was eating the grass and the baby goat said that it was told to eat all of the grass starting in the middle and working its way outward in a circular pattern until it had eaten the grass back down to the acceptable level. I asked, "Who told you to eat all of this grass". The young goat said, "God". Innocence and I left and returned later.

When we came back, the young goat was now full-grown and the fence was a real fence that was made with real posts and real barbed wire. The grass had all been eaten down and was neatly trimmed almost like it had been mowed. The adult goat came over to us and said that it had completed its job and it was time for it to leave. It was a female, a nanny goat. We watched it depart through a gate in the side of the concession. Shortly thereafter a pair of baby goats arrived and the process of eating the grass from the center outward in a circular fashion began all over once again.

I returned later alone, intent on finding where the magic was in this strange concession. The grass was all brown and dry now with its seed tassels rustling in the breeze. Walking in an oval pattern near the outer edges of the concession through the dried rye grass were nine cats all walking upright like people, dressed in matching tan, trench-coats, Fedora hats and dark sunglasses. Six of the felines followed each other at equal distance of about four or five feet, then two more came after a space of ten or twelve feet, then ten or twelve feet further back came the last of the nine cats. They were phantoms. I asked the last of the phantom felines what the meaning and the magic were within concession forty.

The phantom cat said that it was the 'circle of life' and each of the phantom felines represented one of the nine lives of a cat, for everyone knows that cats have nine lives and black cats have always been part and parcel of real magic.

El Tiempo

Last night Innocence and I moved next to concession number forty-two. There was only one thing in the entire concession. It was an elaborate structure comprised entirely of rebar that had been bent and contorted into the framework for a giant tree. There were no people, animals or anything else around. Many of these concessions are really weird.

We sat there staring at this structure for quite a while trying to figure out what the point and purpose of it was. While I was cogitating, it donned on me, that even though I'm familiar with the process that is unfolding here in the Carnival of Magic, perhaps you, the reader, may not be aware or may not appreciate some of its peculiarities. One in particular is the fact that each of these many concessions has a very limited time frame in which it is present before it vanishes and disappears. Most of them last only until I have discovered what and where the magic resides in that concession. Some of them last maybe a few days. The only part of the carnival, which endures is the faded antique sign at the entrance.

Innocence and I left after a while and returned later to see if anything had changed. The framework of rebar was now completely encased in Boxwood vines, as though they had been there for many, many years. The thick vines fused forming the trunk and main branches. It was now a tree made from living vines. In Spanish, Boxwood vines are referred to as, 'Cubre la Tumba', which means, 'to cover the tomb' because these vines are so aggressive and profuse.

The tree of vines was magnificent but I still didn't get it. Then, a very small humanoid looking creature, not much more than twelve inches tall, stepped out from inside or from behind the trunk of the tree. It said that its name was 'El Tiempo' the keeper of time. We might think of him as 'Father Time'. He said that the magic that exists in all things, is time itself for without time, nothing exists.

Tinkerville

I woke up at 1:18 this morning to go to the bathroom. I thought this might be a great time to stop by the Carnival of Magic to continue our quest to visit each of its 107 concessions. Innocence and I went over directly to where number forty-four was located. The place was full of giant Tinker Toys. They immediately began to assemble themselves into all sorts of animals and things. A Tinker Toy pony came up to me and said, "How might I help you?" I asked how was it possible for all of these many pieces to assemble themselves with no one around. The Tinker Toy pony said, " I'm a horse, I'm a cow, I'm a duck, I'm a plow" as it assembled and reassembled itself into one thing after the other.

"It's child's play, it's magic. It's what we do in Toy land. It's what we do here. If an adult wandered in, the whole place falls apart. Adults aren't allowed here.

They've forgot how to fart." The Tinker Toy pony let out a small whinny, then a very big fart.

I asked, "May we enter and take a good look." The pony said, "He can come in, but you look like a Crook." I insisted, "I, myself, am a very old child."

"Magical thinking is what makes our day. If you're a straight thinker, you can't stay and play."

Redwoods

Innocence and I went to concession number forty-seven, last night. It was a big surprise to see that concession alone in the middle of the desert. The whole area of the concession was jammed full of redwood trees. They weren't Giant Sequoia redwoods but mature common redwoods. It was a dense forest. As soon as we stepped into the concession we were completely engulfed in forest and forest sounds. I took Innocence by the hand and told him I didn't want him to get lost there in the forest.

As soon as I did that, a female deer, a doe, appeared from behind the trunk of a large redwood tree. She walked up very close to us. A fawn appeared and then another followed. The doe came closer and closer until our noses touched. She began conversing with us. A large male deer, a stag, came next, then an owl landed in its antlers. Other animals appeared one by one. There was a squirrel, then a raccoon, a skunk, a rabbit, a stellar jay, a fox and a bear then came a woodpecker.

When I would let go of Innocence's hand all of the animals and birds disappeared. They vanished but as soon as I touched his hand again they all reappeared. I guess that gift of telepathy from the dragon worked perfectly just as long as I had contact with a child and his ability to think in magical terms. Magic must actually dwell within the minds of children.

As soon as we left the concession, the redwood forest, along with all of its beautiful creatures vanished, leaving only the pristine desert landscape in its wake.

Swamp Tree

The next night, when Innocence and I went to concession forty-eight, we approached it from an aerial aspect. That has never occurred before. The only thing there was a solitary giant tree that had long thin needles sort of like a conifer but the tree itself didn't look like a pine or spruce or fur tree. It was situated right in the middle of that concession surrounded by swamp water. The entire concession was a swamp. The area close to the base of the trunk was covered in pine needles. Lying out on top of these decaying leaves were what looked like a bunch of small crocodiles. They turned out to be Caiman. We descended down outside the borders of the concession where I suggested to Innocence that he try to make his way across the swamp over to the base of the large tree. The Caiman said that he was welcome because he was a magical creature and a child. They all lined up four wide forming a walkway for him to cross the swamp water over to the trunk of the giant tree.

When it was my turn to cross over, the Caiman said they weren't going to let me cross unless I showed them my magic. I wasn't sure what to do since I'm not a magician with a bag full of tricks to show people. They were going to prevent me from crossing over to the base of the tree where Innocence was now situated. So, I stopped time and went over there anyway. The crocodilians weren't impressed. They had no idea how I managed to do that but they still weren't impressed by it. So, I high stepped it back over the water about six to eight feet above them. That seemed to get their attention and they were finally impressed with my 'magic'. I am not exactly sure what variety of tree the swamp tree was but I think it was a Bald Cypress. We stayed there under the Cypress tree for a while but I still had no idea where the magic was. As we left the concession everything disappeared. There was a little old man sitting in his decrepit rocking chair looking at me. I asked him where the magic resided in concession number forty-eight. He said, "All magic resides in the minds of children", then he too vanished.

Re-Cognition

Hang on to your hat! This will be a wild ride. It was for me. Let me share it with you. As you can see I have been working on this project called the "Art of Magic". This project basically involves two things. The Source gave me 'The Gift of Magic'. When I asked him how I was supposed to use it he said I would have to figure that out on my own. He took me to a place in the middle of the desert, the "Carnival of Magic". It consisted of 107 concessions. My first task was to visit each of these concessions. My second challenge was to figure out where the magic existed in each concession. I have been working my way through these concessions. I have done fifty-five concessions so far. While I was trying to reconcile the magic issue with the swamp and the crocodilians and the old man in the rocking chair, the Source told me I needed to go to 'Nicaragua'.

Nicaragua

Early this morning between 4 and 5 a.m., I was talking with the Source. He told me that I needed to go to Nicaragua. I assure you that Nicaragua was not on any list I had and never was. That is certainly one of the last places on Earth I would ever want to go. I asked him where exactly he wanted me to go and to what time period. He said, "Go now, to the highest mountain in Nicaragua, in 1912, on April the 1st."

I went there through the 'Black Door' because that is what he asked me to do. I ended up in a thick jungle. Through an opening in the branches I could see the peek of the mountain nearby. Hovering maybe fifty feet above it was a large flying saucer. It was making a humming noise. Emitting from the bottom was a horizontally striated pattern of light. It was moving upward from the ground and into the spacecraft like a conveyor belt. It was sucking up people and plants. There may also have been animals picked up as well. For a closer look, I moved my awareness into the spaceship. Inside there were cubicles approximately six feet square arranged around the perimeter of the inside of the craft. Young male and female Indians were being placed into these cubicles along with native plants. There were no children or old people being taken. This was obviously some kind of collecting expedition.

The creatures doing this collecting were very thin and tall, about eight feet more or less. Their heads were shaped like a gourd with the big end on top. They had no visible ears and no noses, just two nostrils. Their heads were attached to their body by a skinny little neck. Their hands had two elastic fingers and an opposing thumb or two all with elliptical flat fingertips. Their fingers were not jointed like ours but seemed to be flexible like rubber. Their eyes were also shaped like a gourd. They appeared to be like the compound eyes of an insect. They had no eyelids and only a tiny little mouth. They had no hair and were all wearing skintight uniforms without any pockets or collars. I wasn't sure what the point was for me to go there in the first place.

Isomer

Last night when I checked in with the Source, he said he wanted me to go back to Nicaragua and set all of the natives free that were imprisoned inside of the spacecraft. I asked him how I was supposed to accomplish that. He said, "Find a way." To travel back in time to April 1st 1912 and to remove an unknown number of captives from inside an alien spaceship full of extraterrestrials hovering fifty feet up in the air above a mountain peak, seemed to be a real stretch for me.

A little over a week ago my son called and said that his daughter told him there was a monster in their swimming pool. I asked what it looked like. His daughter said that it looked like a crocodile or an alligator. I asked how long it had been there. His daughter said about a week. I brought the creature from my son's house in California and put it in my swimming pool because I didn't know what else to do with it. It described itself as the "Embodiment of Crocodilians". The idea that this creature might provide a way to accomplish this particular challenge, needed a name, a name I could work with. It reluctantly agreed to answer to the name "Isomer."

So, with that moniker a plan emerged. Isomer created ten duplicates of itself. I opened a portal directly into the spacecraft. We instantly appeared inside the space ship. The aliens were totally unprepared for eleven huge crocodiles and one giant telepathic shape-shifting black crow to invade their spacecraft and demand the immediate release of all captive humans. The only reasons this endeavor was successful was the element of surprise and the fact that none of these alien beings could distinguish between physical and non-physical reality.

The Nicaraguans were sent back down to the surface by conveyor. The alien spacecraft departed with only plant specimens and no humans and we transported back to my domicile from where we launched our campaign.

I asked this character to go with me over to concession forty-eight. After that I was talking with him trying to connect all of the dots. He told me the following: The little old man sitting in the chair where the swamp tree concession had been located was the caretaker of the Carnival of Magic. His name was Ralph. He was the one that told me magic resides in the mind of a child.

Isomer asked me how old Innocence was. I said about eight years old. He then asked how old my granddaughter Michaela was. She was eight in September. He then asked how many crocodilians were guarding the swamp tree. I said maybe ten or twelve. Then, he asked how many crocodiles rescued the native Nicaraguans. I said, "Ten plus you, that would make it eleven plus a magic crow." He asked when my granddaughter Michaela noticed a giant crocodile in the swimming pool and when did I visit concession forty-eight with the swamp tree and the crocodilians. It was about the same time. Isomer couldn't understand why I had not made the connections. He couldn't understand that I just didn't get "IT". Magic resides in the minds of children. What I had witnessed was magic...pure magic. He couldn't understand, how I was that slow on the draw.

King Fisher

Innocence and I went over to concession fifty-two, last night. As was normal, there was only the one concession standing alone in the middle of the desert. The entire space of the concession was an estuary filled with water, waist deep. Right in the middle of the estuary was a giant, white King Fisher that was as large as an ostrich. It was gobbling up anything and everything it could spear with its long pointed beak. Innocence and I watched this for quite a while trying to figure out where the magic could be found in this concession before we left without a clue.

Several hours later, I returned alone to concession fifty-two. Nothing was there but desert, as though nothing had every actually been there. While walking through the deserted space where the concession had been only hours before, I came upon a roadrunner. It was a little bit large for a roadrunner but it was a roadrunner none-the-less. It stared at me the whole time I was there. I sat down with my legs crossed right in front of it and we had a lengthy conversation. The roadrunner wanted to know what I was doing there and I wanted to know where the magic was in the concession and what was it with the giant King Fisher.

We had a long conversation. The roadrunner told me that the King Fisher was a predator at the top of its food chain just as the roadrunner itself was a top predator in its food chain. It reminded me that it ate insects and spiders, lizards and snakes, eggs and even other birds. It can fly fast and outrun coyotes. When it came to the question of magic, the roadrunner turned out to be a shape-shifting Indian just like the King Fisher had been.

Green Acre

Innocence and I visited concession number thirty-five several times in pursuit of the magic that was contained within it. This concession appeared to be about an acre in size and consisted of rows of green plants that were spaced uniformly. When we first arrived the plants were small and all the same kind. On each subsequent visit the plants grew larger and seemed to no longer be all of the same type. Eventually they all dried up and appeared to be dead or dormant.

In an effort to understand what was going on, I tried several different combinations. When we were both outside the concession we both observed the same things. When we were both inside holding hands the plants appeared as individual clay statues like an army of buried ceramic, Chinese soldiers.

When we were not holding hands, the statues appeared to be animated for Innocence and moved all around interacting with each other but for me they remained immobile statues

When I was outside and Innocence was inside of the concession, the plants appeared to me to be dead and dried up but to Innocence they appeared as row after row of tombstones with names and dates inscribed on them. This baffled me.

Later I returned alone. The concession was gone. There in the middle of the desert where the concession had been, I encountered a large desert tortoise. I presumed that it might in fact not really be a tortoise at all but possibly a shape-shifter so I propped its front end up on a rock and sat down in front of it and engaged it in conversation. That I can assure you was quite revealing.

I asked the tortoise what the point of the concession had been and where the magic lay within it. The tortoise asked me what we had seen and how many rows of plants we saw. There were twenty-six rows of plants when viewed from the front and twenty-six rows when viewed from the side. The tortoise said that added up to 676 plants in all but when viewed from above, which I never thought of, comprised a matrix, a maze and a map. I asked, of course, " A map of what, a matrix for what and what kind of a maze."

The tortoise replied, " The clay statues were replicas of the 676 most important people for you during your lifetime, the ones that have made you who you are." I didn't know what to say so I asked the tortoise if it were a shape shifter. It transformed itself into a short, fat

Indian squaw. She said, "You look surprised!" And I was.

I have always assumed that shape shifters would be men. That is obviously my gender bias. She asked me if I was more comfortable talking to a fat Indian squaw or talking to a tortoise. I told her, "A tortoise" and she once again transformed herself back into the tortoise. She asked me why I was more comfortable talking to a tortoise than a fat Indian squaw. We then continued our discussion.

I told her that I like women. I just don't trust them. They always want something. They are always trying to work some angle. On the other hand, I just don't like guys. I don't like being around them. They are all full of BS. She then asked who had influenced me the most during my lifetime that made me the person I am. "Women...always women. The males were always a bad influence. The women were always right," I said.

The tortoise said, "As you have just witnessed, magic exists only in the mind of a child. Until you can think as a child, see as a child, be as a child, you will never be able to see the magic, work the magic or understand the true nature of magic"

Mountain View

When Innocence and I went to visit concession number thirty-eight, we initially approached it from above to get an overview of the concession before we entered directly into it. The dimensions of the concession were different than most of the others. It was about the same depth but actually occupied the space of almost two concessions because its shape was square, instead of being oblong. As we came down we could clearly see three separate structures. The largest structure was rectangular. Then there was a round one and a smaller square one. The roofs of the structures were all substantial but they had no sides. They were essentially ramadas. The supporting members were all like telephone poles. From the outside there were three ramada-like structures and nothing else. But once we were inside there were a bunch of teenagers running around. We were in the midst of a forest with a mountain visible on one side and a canyon on the other side. It was raining, cold and starting to snow.

There was one older male about forty who was wearing a tee shirt with no sleeves. His hair was short and balding on top. The scene was chaotic at best. I could not reconcile in my mind the two drastically different scenes between inside and outside the concession.

Later I returned to where concession thirty-eight had been only hours before. Nothing was there but virgin desert and a lone coyote sitting in the midst of where the concession had been. I was sure that this coyote must be a shape-shifter. I walked right up to the coyote and engaged it in conversation. I didn't bother asking it where the concession had gone but I did want to know where the magic was located.

"When you were outside of the concession you

could only see its structure but when you entered the concession holding on to the hand of the young boy, you were exposed not to his imagination but to what he envisioned. You mistakenly think a child imagines things when in actuality they envision them and any thing envisioned becomes their reality. That is the very essence of magic. If you can envision something it can become reality", said the wily coyote.

Desert Jungle

Last night Innocence and I visited concession number forty-one. Once again we approached the concession from above to get an overview before we actually entered the concession itself. That way we might be able to devise a plan on how to escape if it were deemed necessary or prudent to do so. From directly above, the concession appeared to be a small patch of jungle right in the middle of the desert.

Once inside things looked much different. There was a path that led down the hill to a giant river like the Amazon. Dense jungle surrounded us completely. The Jungle was alive with threatening sounds and animal activity. My first thought was that I didn't want to loose contact with Innocence so I had him climb on my back with his legs around my waist and his arms around my neck. That way my hands were free to ward off any attacks from unknown creatures in the jungle.

Our first encounter was with a huge snake. It was an

Anaconda, a really big one. It told me that it ate small children and would never die. Fortunately for us, the snake had poor eyesight and didn't see Innocence on my back. I told the snake that I heard several small children playing down by the river and the snake slithered off down the trail to the river.

The next animal we encountered was a hungry tiger. I told the Tiger that the Anaconda had just left to go eat some small children down by the river. I told the tiger that the snake said that it was the king of the jungle and would never die. The Tiger growled under his breath and said, " So he thinks he is the king of the jungle. We will see about that." He too then disappeared down the trail leading to the river.

Our next visitor was a male Elephant. He was looking for his lost herd. I told him that they were down by the river. Next a fat Orangutan waddled up.

He was headed down to the river. I told him that would be unwise. He squinted at us through his little beady eyes and said anyone with two heads must be very wise. He turned around and climbed back up into the jungle trees.

I was getting the idea. I was getting the hang of envisioning things like a child does. They become very real in every sense. He even smelled like an old Orangutan.

Thieves Throttle

Innocence and I visited concession forty-three next. We approached it from the side in the more or less customary way. It was a quaint little store with an Old English touch like something out of a scene from a 'Harry Potter' movie. It was completely surrounded by cobblestone roads. The hand-painted wooden sign above the door read 'Purser Shoppe'. As we entered the concession, shoppers seemed to emerge from every corner. An entire Old English town now surrounded the shop. It was complete with busy shoppers on cobblestone streets that wandered off in several directions.

Once inside Innocence asked about a purse or pouch that hangs around your neck under your shirt to carry valuables. He seemed to have no difficulty conversing with the shopkeepers. I on the other hand couldn't understand a word they were saying. It appeared that the shop made purses, pouches and sacks for carrying things, out of leather and fine silks.

A sample of silk fabric hanging from a hook on the wall got my attention. It was a rose-colored pink on one side and a dark purplish-blue on the other side. I reached out and grasped it between my fingers and rubbed it back and forth to feel its quality. Everyone gasped and stared at me. The shopkeeper came over to me and asked some questions but I couldn't understand what he was saying. He pointed at the material then at some purses hanging from racks on the wall. I shook my head no and walked away.

Innocence picked out a nice leather pouch and proceeded to procure it in the strangest of ways. The shopkeeper wrote the price down on a small square of parchment paper. It just said 25 and then had some sign next to it but I don't know what amount the sign indicated. It could have been for pounds or guineas or farthings, maybe even for something else. That was it. The shopkeeper then put that small piece of paper in a little wooden chest with a domed lid and closed it. Everyone kept looking at me the whole time in the strangest of ways.

When we left the shop Innocence put his purse around his neck and buttoned his blouse-like white shirt. I noticed something was around my neck. It was a purse made of that pink and blue silk. The cords on it seemed to be alive. They were shrinking. I couldn't get the thing off. I tried to cut the cords but my knife didn't touch them. I don't know what they were made of. I immediately went back to where the concession had been but now it was gone. Ralph, the little old caretaker had no idea where the concession was and had no idea how I could get rid of the purse around my neck. He said that I needed to find someone who knew how to get rid of it before it choked me to death. This had to be bad magic of some kind.

My first thought was Merlin the magician. He is a friend of mine. I immediately transported over to Ireland where Merlin had been working and dragged him out of his tree in the middle of the night. He said,

"That looks like a 'Thieves Throttle'. What did you try to steal this time?"

I told Merlin that I didn't try to steal anything. I just touched some silk cloth hanging on the wall and the shopkeeper tried to get me to buy it but I wasn't interested.

Merlin said, "Don't you know, if you touch it, you buy it. If you leave without it, you stole it because they can't sell it to anyone else. That's deep magic. I don't know how to break that spell, the 'Thieves Throttle'. Maybe Morgan might know. She is into spells and all that stuff. Give her my regards but be careful, very careful around her. I speak from experience." From there I transported to her cave.

I caught her off guard. She wasn't impressed with my story. Morgan said she had no way to break a spell like that without knowing exactly who and when and why it was cast as well as what techniques were used in the casting of it. I was on my own. No one was going to get me out of this jam except me, myself. I took the 'Black Door' back in time to before I touched the cloth and didn't touch anything. The spell was never cast. The 'Thieves Throttle' vanished from around my neck. I could once again breathe free and easy, me, myself and I.

Tempest Mountain

Last night was the last full moon of December. Magic Crows gather somewhere for every full moon. All magic crows are shape-shifting sorcerers. I was King of Magical Crows at one time. They Black-balled me and threw me out of the International Murder of Magical Crows when I became a wizard. Sorcerers and wizards don't see eye to eye. They don't get along. They don't play well together. I have kept in contact with one magic crow. She lives in the seventeen hundreds on the Normandy coast where English is still spoken. I went to where she was last night at the full moon gathering. It turned out to be on Tempest Mountain in New Zealand. An island volcano blew up there in New Zealand a few days ago. Several tourists were killed. You have to be careful around volcanoes.

I went over to where she was through the 'Black Door'. That method is fast, easy and very clean. When I arrived, my friend the magic crow told me that she had to ruffle my feathers because all of the other crows had a hard time getting to Tempest Mountain because of turbulent winds, dust and volcanic ash. Their feathers were all dusty and tattered. They would easily notice my smooth clean feathers and discover my presence. I told her that she would have to lead me around because if I opened my eyes everyone would know that I was not a sorcerer and didn't belong there.

Magic crows have eyes that are all coal black, while wizards eyes glow fiery red. I squinted so she could see. She was quite surprised and asked, " You haven't been dabbling in magic have you, because your eyes are turning a sapphire blue?"

I told her I was working on a project that involved the 'art of magic'. Magicians, you see, have eyes that are sapphire blue. You can always tell if someone is a sorcerer, a wizard or a magician by the colors of their eyes.

Vantage Point

This was a very interesting project. It began a week ago and involved several separate steps to get to the 'Vantage Point'. The first thing that happened was the Source said, "Michael, get on my shoulders." That had never happened before. He helped me up onto his shoulders. He then asked me what I saw so I told him. He then said, "Because you are sitting on my shoulders you can see farther than you could before. Now you can see beyond the Event horizon."

It was true. I could see beyond the Event Horizon. A couple of nights later the Source said that he wanted me to stand on his shoulders, so I did. He said that he would hold my feet so that I would be stable and not fall down and he did. He said that I should be able to see even farther now while standing on his shoulders than I could while sitting on his shoulders and I could. Not only could I see past the Event Horizon but I could also see beyond the curvature of the earth. Before, the area beyond the Event Horizon dropped down and away as the surface of the earth curved downward. Now the area beyond the Event Horizon curved upwards and was easy for me to see.

A couple of nights later the Source said that I no longer needed to stand on his shoulders to see beyond the Event Horizon because I could go to that position on my own because I knew its location. We had a long discussion about not only seeing the future Event Horizon but also seeing the 'past' Event Horizon which in essence gave birth to the future event or outcome of the past event. That was tricky but it didn't take too long to get the hang of it.

The next step in the process involved not only facing forward and backwards but also facing to the right and to the left at the same time. Not only did the space beyond the future Event Horizon curve upwards but the space behind the past Event Horizon curved upward and the space on both sides curved upward as well revealing several striations connecting the past event with its future event. The striations arced from the past to the future in a curve. Arcs on the left side were the possibilities and arcs on the right side were their probabilities. I was located in the focal point of a parabolic bowl. The Source said that not only would I now be able to see future events coming but also the specifics of the origins of those events in the past and the different possible arcing pathways connecting them. This he called the 'Vantage Point.'

Water Fall

Innocence and I visited concession number forty-five twice. The first time we approached it from ground level. It was essentially a waterfall pouring down out of the sky into the desert. A lot of water was coming down but it didn't go anywhere. There was a pool of water at the bottom but no stream exiting from it. The whole thing looked so surreal and out of place in the middle of the desert, I decided to return another day after I had given it some thought on how best to evaluate this strange phenomenon.

The second time we went, we approached from an elevated position in order to determine the source of the water that seemed to appear out of thin air. That shouldn't be possible. As we entered the concession's space, I held Innocence's hand for two reasons. First of all, I didn't want anything to happen to him and second I wanted to see what was happening more like a child would see it. When we stepped inside the concession, a panorama appeared that was complete with a stream, towering cliffs, mountains in the distance and riparian vegetation.

Innocence decided to go swimming. On the edge of the pool of water near the back on the left side sat a tiny little character of some kind. I knew it wasn't a leprechaun because it was larger than that. It didn't look like a fairy though they come in different sizes. I made my way over and engaged it in conversation. I couldn't understand what it was saying so I picked it up and placed it on my left shoulder. It turned out to be a Gnome. I asked it what its name was and it said it answered to the name Gem though that wasn't its given name. When I asked Gem to explain to me the magic behind what I was experiencing, the waterfall and entire scene itself became glowing golden outlines comprised of tiny balls that moved along gossamer thin strings. The substance of everything had disappeared. I asked Gem what it was that I was seeing. He said that it was the intent of everything there. The substance of everything was created of pure illusion, illusion that he had created not illusion like a mirage in the summer heat of the desert. The third critical element was magical thinking like a child has. You have been given the gift of illusion. That doesn't mean seeing things that aren't there but actually making things that aren't there, seem to be there, real enough to touch, real enough to walk on, real enough to fool anyone including yourself.

Cow Pies

The next concession that Innocence and I visited was concession number forty-six. Right in the middle of the desert was a large red barn with a tall silo surrounded by lush green pasture filled with Holstein cows, no bulls, no calves, just full grown black and white cows. Near the fence stood an old farmer holding a wooden pitchfork. I asked him what was going on. He said, "Milken time."

The big black and white cows ambled into the barn one at a time full and left out the other end empty. I asked about calves. He said, "Got none."

"How about bulls?" I said.

"None of them either."

"Why not?" I asked.

"Them cows are all magic. They don't need no calves nor no bulls. They just keep turning that green grass into milk and cream and cheese. Now that is magic if there ever were any."

I didn't know what to say.

"And them 'cow pies' makes grass grow any where, even here in the middle of the desert."

Menorah Menagerie

Innocence and I visited concession number forty-nine next. There seems to be this never-ending series of surprises each time we visit a new concession. This one was no exception. It was no larger than a square foot in size. There was a tiny stream of water flowing here and there throughout that small space. I told Innocence to stand back and keep an eye on everything that transpired while I shrank myself down and down until I vanished into that tiny concession. It was a fantastic water-park with pairs of small, I mean really small, characters all over the place. They were scurrying about from booth to booth decked out in their colorful attire. They didn't look like anyone or anything I have ever encountered before. They all stared at me like I didn't belong there and I didn't.

The booths were large and small, elaborate or simple. All were elegant, all were colorful and all had menorahs. Four lights, then one, then four more, all shining brightly in the darkness of the night, illuminating the entire park and its sparkling water attractions. I couldn't believe what I was seeing.

I returned to my original full size and asked Innocence if he had witnessed anything. He was very excited and said, "I saw everything through your eyes. It was pure magic. The magic of shared vision."

I said, " But why so many menorahs?" Then

Innocence reminded me, "Last night was the first night of Hanukkah."

Festival of Lights

Last night Innocence and I visited the adjacent concession, number fifty-one. Nothing was there but virgin desert where that concession was supposed to be. As soon as we stepped into the concession's space, we found ourselves right in the middle of a town straight from the Middle Ages of Europe. Cobblestone streets narrow and steep, were lined with two story gray-stone shops where keepers lived above and bartered their wares below. Lights of all kinds were everywhere. The whole town was brightly lit but not by streetlights, not by bulbs, not by neon's, not by candles, flames nor fire but by magic, pure magic like I have never seen before. It was fantastical. There were no people anywhere. So, we popped into what might be thought of as a depot.

The space inside was huge compared to the structure itself we just entered. It was reminiscent of an ancient train-terminal, dark and poorly lit with walnut-paneled walls and few if any windows. No chairs or benches, just cold hard marble floors and a long dark counter behind which a single official in a drab uniform stood. I approached this scowling lady and asked her about the magical lights outside and the absence of crowds.

She said sternly, " They were just here looking for you. You were nowhere to be found."

I of course wanted to know who had been looking for me.

She replied, "Why, Death, of course, along with all his helpers."

I then asked what was going on with all the bright lights. I had no interest in 'my death'. I much prefer 'my life' and living it.

She then gave me the look reserved for idiots and the like and replied, "The Festival of Lights."

Later, I asked the Source how it was possible for 'Death' not to be able to find me.

The Source said, "You were talking with me. When you are with me no one can ever find you!"

I asked about the magical lights. The Source said, "It is Hanukkah, you know."

Yo Kai

What is a YoKai, you might ask. It is the spirit of a dearly departed person that has combined with the spirit of an animal or inanimate object or thing, which also is no longer living. They were created or connected by a traumatic death. Each YoKai acquires a unique name and each YoKai has special gifts or powers. They are invisible but create all kinds of challenges and influence us in our every day lives.

'Magnifico' is a YoKai. He is the character that was referred to in "Isomer" (p.129). First I will give you a brief history of 'Magnifico' then, I will tell you how I became involved with him. Last of all I will share with you his contribution to the health and well being of our family. Three or four weeks ago, my son who lives in Orange County called and said, " There is a monster in our pool."

I of course wanted to know what it was and how long it had been there, what it looked like and what it was doing. My son asked his daughter, who can actually see YoKai. She said that it looked sort of like a crocodile. It had been in their pool since the chlorine generator stopped working and the pool turned green. My son told me to, "Get rid of it!" So later that night, a bit after midnight, I went over to his house and located the strange creature. It looked sort of like an alligator and sort of like a crocodile. I told the creature that it couldn't stay. It had to go. I didn't know what to do with it so I took it home with me and put it in our swimming pool. I told it not to bother anyone and to leave our dogs alone. Eventually I discovered that it was in fact, a YoKai.

His name was Frank. Everyone in his family called him Frankie. He was on vacation in Egypt when he accidentally fell overboard off of a ferry into the river Nile. A giant crocodile swallowed him whole. The local authorities shot the giant crocodile that was named "Magnificient" by the locals, in a futile effort to rescue Frankie. The traumatic deaths of Frankie and the giant crocodile 'Magnificent', created 'Magnifico', which was a crocodile with the arms and legs of a man, Frankie.

A couple of weeks later, my son called from the beach, where his daughter was having her weekly surfing lesson. Her surfing instructor brought her back to the beach complaining that she wouldn't do anything, just sit there in the water on her surf- board. His daughter told the instructor that the cat scratched her and the salt water was burning the cut. Later she told my son that her surfboard was talking to her and told her that she was going to be hit on the head by the board and drown so she didn't want to surf anymore that day. Subsequently she volunteered that the crocodile monster was back in their swimming pool.

Now it was my challenge to try to find out what really happened. It seemed highly unlikely to me that her surfboard actually talked to her let alone foretell the future. So, I constructed a time line to put all of the elements of the story into proper perspective.

In the morning before my granddaughter's surfing

lesson my wife was very concerned about her safety. "Magnifico" the YoKai must have sensed my wife's concern and returned to my son's house and accompanied my granddaughter to the beach in the afternoon to keep an eye on her. The YoKai must have accompanied her when she went out into the ocean. She thought that her surfboard was talking to her but it was actually the Yokai "Magnifico", the crocodilliman who saved her from certain death by drowning, in the turbulent ocean surf.

Aladdin's Palace

Last night Innocence and I ventured over to where concession number fifty-three was supposed to be located.There was nothing in the concession's space but a desert.I began looking around for any signs that something had actually been there. In the front corner on the left side I found a small metal cylinder about the size of a #404 can of beans.It was smooth and cold, shiny and light, like a cylinder of buffed aluminum. In both of the back two corners of where the concession should have been, I found two more metal cylinders. I crisscrossed the space back and forth several times looking for anything out of the ordinary. There was nothing in the front right hand corner.Along the edge of the left side I found a small ball of gelatin-like stuff and on the back edge I found two more of these blobs of gelatin, the size of tennis balls. I put a ball of gelatin on top of each of the metal cylinders located in all three of the corners.Then, Innocence and I approached the concession space from outside the other front corner. As we stepped into the space, we were engulfed by desert.Not just any desert but a dry sandy desert, like the Sahara Desert. We found ourselves inside of a compound with sandstone walkways surrounding a sandstone palace.We made our way inside this palace.

We found no one inside. The rooms were all poorly illuminated. We wondered around from room to room looking for anyone we could find. Out of a back room emerged my granddaughter. She is the same age as Innocence. I left them there together to explore the insides of the palace while I sought answers elsewhere. I asked them to hold hands so no one would get lost until I returned.

When I came back they told me that there were hidden tunnels in the walls of every room. These tunnels were what they called 'Story Tunnels'. When you stepped into one of them you became engulfed as a player/participant in one of the many adventures of Aladdin. This place was Aladdin's Magical Palace. I asked them how many tunnels they thought there were in Aladdin's palace. My granddaughter thought there were maybe thirteen or fourteen. Innocence thought there were eighteen. I counted twenty-six.

I believe the greater your imagination, the more 'Story Tunnels' you find in a Magical Palace.

The Garden

While I was conversing with the Source last night, he asked me to 'walk with him'.When we stopped, he asked me what I saw.I saw nothing. He proceeded to tell me that this was a garden. A yellow line like you would see on a paved street appeared.He asked me what I saw.I saw a single yellow line stretching from where I was standing off into the distance, splitting the space into two sides, the left side and the right side.The rest was blackness.

The Source then proceeded to rotate my field of vision ninety degrees creating a horizontal yellow line. He asked me to describe what I saw. I told him I saw a horizontal yellow line separating two areas of blackness, one near and the other far. He then rotated my field of vision an additional ninety degrees and asked me what I saw.

I saw a single yellow line stretching from where I was standing off into the distance, splitting the space in half. The rest was blackness.

The Source said, " Now the left side is on your right and the right side is on your left. How are you going to distinguish between them?"

I replied, "This one is here and that one is there." Then, the Source proceeded to rotate my field of vision an additional ninety degrees and he asked, " How are you going to distinguish between them now."

I said, " Top and bottom."

The Source then asked, " How do you plan to

differentiate top from far, near from bottom, left from here and right from there." He then removed the yellow line and continued, " This is a garden, the 'Garden of Good and Evil'. Anything you plant here will grow." He removed a small seed from his pocket and planted it. That seed sprouted and grew into a plant that produced a single tulip-like flower.

He asked, " How do you determine if the fruit of this flower will be good or evil. All things are either good or evil. Desire for a 'good' outcome does not justify the use of an evil means to accomplish it. Killing an unborn child is evil. Inconvenience cannot justify it."

Flower Garden

Last night Innocence and I went to concession number fifty-four. It was located directly across the central walkway from concession fifty-three. In front there were two vertical wood poles that supported an ornately decorated sign with two words on it, 'Flower Garden'. Around the perimeter there was a short, filigreed-fence about fourteen inches high. The decorative fence and the fancy sign were both white-washed. The letters were of pastel colors. From the outside looking in, there was the continuation of desert vegetation but from the inside everything changed.

Innocence and I entered beneath the sign holding hands. There were flowers everywhere. Not in vases but on vines and bushes, on trees and in the ground. We followed an inlayed stone pathway. The varieties and colors were fantastic. Coming to greet us down the path from the opposite direction was my granddaughter. We all held hands as she proudly showed us all the many varieties and spectacular specimens throughout the concession. It was truly magical. How could all of these delicate tropical plants exist in the middle of a hot, dry desert?

One an...Other

The next concession we visited was number fifty-five. It was quite a sight. The entire space was glass. The walls were all crystal clear glass at least twelve feet high. Even the roof was clear glass, flat glass. It was like a giant clear glass rectangular box. There were no doors and no windows, only solid plate glass with no wood or steel super structure to support it. We walked all around it but couldn't find any way to enter. The whole thing was filled with mirrors, not just any shaped mirrors but vertical segments arranged so that you couldn't see anything inside but mirrors.

The way we finally got into the place was through a ventilation stack on the roof. It was sort of like a chimney. We slid down the chimney like Santa Clause would. It was very strange inside. The mirrors were all arranged so that it was impossible to see out of the building and it was impossible to see yourself. You could only see someone else, some other person. I could see Innocence and Innocence could see me but it was impossible for us to see our selves. The point of this concession was obviously to force you to stop focusing on yourself and start to focus on others, there in lies the magic of this place.

Hemp Rope

Fifty-six was next on the list for us to visit. I asked Innocence to get up on my shoulders because I had a feeling that this concession might be weird. Innocence and I were surprised at what we found when we got there. All around the perimeter of the concession was a large hemp rope. It was about one and a quarter inches in diameter. We walked around it several times looking for a splice where two ends would be joined together. We couldn't find any.

We tried everything we could think of to get the concession to operate, but to no avail: Innocence was on my shoulders, then not on my shoulders; We walked together then separately; We went inside the rope together then separately; We held hands; We crawled; We walked on the rope itself like a tight rope. Nothing worked. Finally I asked Innocence to go outside the concession area and observe to see if anything occurred. I sat down it the middle and meditated on the problem.

After awhile spirit-animals began to arrive. The first was a coyote then a jackrabbit. Next a skunk, a raccoon, a bobcat and a badger arrived. A bear, a fox and a wolf came. Birds started to arrive. A hawk an owl a turkey and raven came. They kept coming and coming. They arranged themselves in a semicircle facing me. They shared the mystery and magic of the desert with me. One said the rope represented the circle of life, another said that it separated the spirit world of Native Americans from the physical world. I was anxious to hear what Innocence had observed on the outside of the hemp rope. When I asked, he said that he fell asleep and didn't see any thing.

Imanges

We moved on last night to concession number fifty-seven. There we encountered Imanges. What is that you ask? It is the name I gave to these strange things we encountered. You perhaps might know them by some other names. We approached the concession from above.

In the middle of the concession space there was a rectangle of these Imanges approximately the size of a single car garage, ten or twelve feet wide by twenty to twenty-two feet long. These things were small ropes suspended in air by an invisible force. One end of the ropes seemed to be attached to an invisible flat ceiling about twelve feet high. There were several different items strung onto the ropes about six inches apart from top to bottom. The bottoms ended with a knot and were three to four feet above the surface of the floor. Each one of these strung objects was unique. There must have been thousands of them hanging there. I had no idea what they were or what they could be used for. I was told that they were magical items, which could chase away evil spirits and break magic spells. I didn't believe either of those things.

Subsequently I encountered two witches who didn't look like witches but I knew that they were. They had a totally flat bush that was absolutely black and leafless. They were using it to cast a spell on me. I grabbed one of these Imanges and ran towards them. Not only the bush but the witches themselves totally disintegrated in a shower of sparks when I touched them with one of these magical hanging ropes. They must have very powerful magic.

I grabbed a bunch of these hanging Imanges and strung them up all around my house, my office, my son's house and my family's as well. It is never a bad idea to get rid of any evil spells or creatures if you ever have the chance to do so.

Ant Lion

Innocence and I visited concession number fifty-eight, last night. It was reminiscent of an open-pit copper mine that was perfectly round with spiraling steps down to the bottom at the center. Each spiral was about sixteen inches wide and eight to ten inches high.

I didn't know if it would be better to walk around the spiral steps or to go straight down to the bottom across each spiral like a stairs. Both seemed to be rather risky with an eight-year old in tow.

When we were most of the way down the spiral steps I looked back up the steep slope we just walked down. The spiral steps were gone. In their place was sand. Down below us in the center there was some kind of large creature stirring. It had giant pincer-like mandibles. This thing was mostly buried under the sand with its two scissor like mandibles protruding from beneath the soft sand. It reminded me of a giant ant lion and we apparently were would-be ants.

Where was the magic in this place? How were we going to get out of here? By what machination were the steps turned into sand? The answer had to be here somewhere. It always is. Then it dawned on me. The sand may not be sand at all but instead the 'sands of time'. I can stop time. What will happen if I do? So, I did. The spiral stairs re-appeared. I can change my size in the twinkle of an eye. I grabbed Innocence and enlarged myself. Plop we were out. The lion was squashed in the process. It was no match for my giant foot. I looked around. I wasn't a giant at all. Somehow we had been shrunk down into the world of the ant lion. That is powerful magic.

Tic...Tic...Tock

Last night Innocence and I went to concession number fifty-nine. It was standing alone in the midst of a desert. I asked Innocence to wait outside and tell me what he observed later, as I entered the concession on my own.

The entire concession space was an elaborate fancy ballroom filled with large round dining tables set in exquisite style with white linens and beautiful china, crystal and silver dinnerware. The place was immaculate. The high ceiling was illuminated with extravagant chandeliers. No servants were there. Guests had not yet arrived. I sat down at one of the tables and poured myself a tall glass of deep, red burgundy wine. As I was admiring the expensive wine a shaft of light impinged upon my glass. It was squashed almost flat, thin and wide. Momentarily it returned to its original shape with no loss of wine and no damage to its crystalline flute. Moments later the process repeated itself. I had no idea what was happening. I can't even begin to imagine what could possibly create effects like that.

Later I asked Innocence what he witnessed. He said that he saw a sliver of white light slice right through the dining area, instantaneously cutting through everything then disappearing to where it came from. I was baffled. I had no idea the source of such strange magic.

In our world the definition of a 'tic' is: A compulsive sound or movement that's difficult to control. The

Source finally provided me with an explanation of what I had just experienced. He said that the 'tic' originated from the 'Seventh String'. Our string happens to be number five. There are twenty-six strings in total. Each has its own separate time, timing, dimensions, density and reality. They all occupy the same space simultaneously but have different qualities. When one string moves through another, sometimes there is interference created. When one time stream impinges upon another and they are both at their crest or trough (i.e. the timing in one string matches the timing in another string) even though their frequencies are different, like the same note played simultaneously from different octaves, can re-enforce each other.

After all, in magic, timing is everything. Black magic originates in the third string. Tics in our string originate from the seventh string when the tocks of time match perfectly. We see that as the flash of light and the change in dimensions of things. All true magic originates in strings outside of ours.

Black Board...

Jungle...Mumble...Grumble...
Stumble...Fumble...Rumble...
Crumble...Tumble...Jumble...

Who knows, who cares? What did we find at concession number sixty. We went there three times.

I thought I might find something different the second or third time but things were exactly the same. It was a schoolroom for sixty, first graders. There were three blackboards on the front wall, six rows of ten desks each, two corkboards on the right side separated by a single entrance door. The left side had short cabinets along the entire wall made of birch wood. Nothing was made from plastic. Single-pane windows along the wall above the cabinetry would open for ventilation. There was a large circular clock above the middle blackboard with its giant second hand moving infinitesimally slowly, surely towards escape, when the red clangor, high above the door rattled your brains and damaged your hearing. I was surprised by the absence of a desk for the teacher. There were the familiar white chalk, the row of erasers, ready for throwing and the wood pointer with its black rubber tip for poking eyes out and head whacking.

There was no sink, no bathroom, no pictures on the walls. The desks were small with a square space under the seats for stuffing things into, (your stuff if you were lucky). I didn't have to look hard for the magic in this place. This place turned me into a crazy little kid who never grew up. It was magic at its best. I learned to count. I learned to sit still, sort of.

I learned to read and that has made all the difference and that has set me free.

Director's Chair

We moved on to the next concession on our 'to do' list. It was number sixty-one. There wasn't any thing there but plain desert. The point of this whole project has been to understand the true nature of Magic. Each concession has been challenging for me to find the magic hidden therein. This one was no exception. On the contrary, this was by far the most difficult one of all.

I walked all around it and all over it but I just wasn't getting it. I walked. I talked. I crawled. I sat. I meditated. Finally I got a folding chair made of wood and canvas, a director's chair. I sat and sat until I finally began to put all of the pieces together.

This involved time, timing, vision, imagination, intuition, telepathy, time travel and the innocence of a child combined with their ability to think and see things in magical terms. When I finally assembled all of the pieces to the puzzle, this is what was there.

It was a B-17, not just any B-17 but one that flew many successful bombing missions in Europe during World War II, crashed landed with wheels up, didn't burn and all of its crew members survived that crash and the entire war uninjured. They were all lined up in front of their B-17 saluting me. Magic!

Pure Magic!

The Fart

Innocence and I went to concession number sixty-two several times. I was completely baffled by what happened there. It was kaleidoscope-nonsense. Nothing made any sense to me. Event by event, it was totally incoherent.

In the middle of the night I was awakened by a fart, not a big one, not a loud one, not a juicy one but one so noxious it awoke me from my deep slumber. I assure you that had never happened to me before. It must have been magic. It was one of those eureka moments, for in an instant I got it. I finally got it. I instantly knew where the magic resided in this concession. All of the weirdness and absurdity of the kaleidoscopic menagerie became perfectly clear, lucid and logical. Whoever designed and created these magical concessions must have really known what they were doing.

Each and every one of the sights, sounds and events that flew past me in my ignorance were all associated with specific smells. You never forget a smell. You never forget where and when you first encountered it. A smell instantly gets your attention. It transports you to another time, another place, or another reality, even a magical one.

Putting Green

Innocence and I visited concession sixty-three, last night. The entire concession space was covered in green grass, putting-green grass with a single pin, a single hole and a single flag with the number one on it, sticking up out of the hole. We walked all over the concession. It was a rectangular golf green that was approximately forty feet by sixty feet in size. The grass was superb. It was perfect for putting. One oddity I noticed was that the entire surface of the green was sloped slightly in towards the cup.

You had to get down on ground level to appreciate the slope. It was designed to help players be successful rather than designed for failure. I got two putters and some practice balls so Innocence and I could try out the putting green. It was nice, really nice. It was smooth with a predictable grain. It was a real pleasure to make some long putts. It took me quite awhile to figure out where the magic lay in this concession but I finally figured it out.

Life is a game, like golf is a game. The magic is in the playing of the game to the best of your ability. The secret is in the showing up. It's your life. It's your game, so it's really important that you show up.

Hall of Dates

Last night when Innocence and I went to the next concession, number sixty-four, nothing was there, absolutely nothing. But, as soon as we stepped over the edge into the concession space, we were inside a hall. It looked like a dance hall, sort of. It occupied the entire concession space. The ceiling was high. The floor was shiny, smooth and beautiful. There were no doors and no windows anywhere. There was no furniture, no tables and no chairs. No one was there, nothing was happening. It reminded me of a place where events would take place. We walked all around the building looking for some key to understanding exactly what this concession was all about. Then, I saw a small curtain covering a tiny alcove. Behind the curtain sitting on a mushroom-like stool was a bald-headed elf in front of some kind of a console.

I pulled back the curtain and asked if he were an elf. He said that he was. I asked him what kind of elf he was. He said that he was an Entertainment Elf and his name was Phillip. I asked Phillip what he was doing and what kind of console was he operating. He showed me what the console was capable of. It had three sections. One section was for selecting a date. Another section was to enter the type of event it was i.e. a dance or game, musical or symphony, concert or perhaps something else. The third section was for specific decorations and attendees, which came directly from the subconscious mind of the individual activating the concession. In order to initiate this whole process the only thing necessary was to enter the date of a specific event. Then, the place was essentially transformed into a holodeck, a giant hologram constructed from the subconscious mind of the observer.

Play Castle

The place Innocence and I went to last night reminded me of one of McDonalds' play castles, only much more elaborate. It was almost thirty feet high, three stories, sitting right in the middle of the space where concession number sixty-five was supposed to be. It was completely surrounded by water on all sides, very colorful, ornately decorated, designed to catch the eye of every child. It was as inviting as the gingerbread house from the fairy tale of Hansel & Gretel. There was only one doorway in the front of the castle. When Innocence and I held hands, a floating pathway appeared that lead to the front door. Of course, we immediately walked across the water, up the single step and right into the castle.

The insides were immense. It was reminiscent of the inside of a parking garage, poorly illuminated, empty and gray. On the far side there was a little old man sitting in a swivel chair, nothing else. I asked Innocence to stay where he was while I went to check out the stranger in the swivel chair. I was certainly surprised when I got there.

That little old man was I, myself. I asked him what this place was. He said, "This is the place of premonition. That is the heart of magic. All magic is premonition. The magician always knows what will happen before it happens. It is created in this place, in this space, practiced and rehearsed until ready to be delivered in an instant through the mind's eye of a child into the eye of the unprepared observer. Magic is nothing more than illusion turned into reality."

I sat down into that chair where I was already sitting. The whole space was instantly transformed into a kaleidoscope of magic.

Sixty-Six

Innocence and I visited concession number sixty-six next. The entire concession space was covered with a thick cement slab. On top of the slab was this thing that looked sort of like a tall, round pointed building. The base was about thirty-eight feet in diameter. It was sort of like a segmented cone with four or five sections each of diminishing size. The sides of each cone tapered inward from bottom to top. The thing was at least ninety feet tall. Sitting in front of it was a carnie yelling out, "Get your tickets here. Get your tickets now. Get your tickets for the space ride of your life." He was a strange-looking little man with funny ears and a tiny nose.

We got our tickets and passed through a diminutive

door into a small elevator with sloping sides about four feet wide and less than thirty inches in depth. It took us up a couple of stories, then opened into a round room filled with reclining chairs. I counted the chairs. There were twenty-two of them arranged in a circle. Innocence and I got into a couple of seats. The people behind us in line arrived next and sat down on the other side of the room. It was a young lady with her daughter who appeared to be four or five years old. Before too long the lights dimmed and the ride began. There were noises and jiggling, sensations of movement. I was wondering exactly how this whole ride would compare to rides in Disneyland. I don't know for some reason I fell asleep momentarily. I awoke with a jerk and wondered what I had missed. I looked over towards Innocence. He was gone. I got up and walked around. The young lady and her daughter on the other side of the room were fast asleep. I went looking for Innocence.

I found him in the control room with a couple of other small kids. When I got closer I noticed they weren't kids at all but two small aliens with funny ears and tiny noses. We were in a spaceship heading into outer space. I went downstairs looking for other people. In the floors below where we had been there were cages filled with several different kinds of animals. The only other people beside Innocence and me were the young lady and her daughter. This was a hunting expedition. These two space aliens abducted us. The only magic left in this concession was the magic I was going to use on these two knuckleheads who thought they could pull off this caper.

Little did they suspect that this child sitting next to them was neither a child nor a human but a magical creature with powers they could not even imagine, powers that would soon be unleashed upon them, like lightning in the dead of night.

Alfalfa

When Innocence and I visited concession number sixty-Seven last night, we found nothing but a field of small plants. The field was more than twice the size of most concessions, which are roughly sixty by ninety feet. This one was more like one hundred and twenty by two hundred and twenty feet in size. These little plants were green like grass but I wasn't exactly sure what they actually were. We went there several times. Each time when we re-visited the concession we found something different. The second time we went the plants were much larger.

The next time we went after that, the plants had all been cut down and were furrowed into several long rows. When we went the time after that there were bales of green hay strewn haphazardly over the entire field. That was when I realized that the plants were actually alfalfa and these bales of hay were green, alfalfa-hay.

The last time we re-visited concession sixty-seven

there was nothing there but a giant silo standing in the middle of open, dry, dirt. It clearly showed the magic that turns sunlight into food for animals, that in turn give us food and clothing, that give us life, the greatest magic of all.

Coal

I asked the Source last night which project I should work on next. He told me to continue working through the concessions in the Carnival of Magic but, he added, "Don't take Innocence with you on concession sixty-eight," which was the very next one on my to- do list. That seemed odd because he usually reminds me to be sure and take Innocence along with me. That request became perfectly clear.

Concession number sixty-eight was as black as black can be. I mean it was completely black. It was covered with coal dust and had a giant chunk of coal larger than a car sitting right in the middle. It took me several trips to finally figure out that the huge black thing in the middle of the concession was actually an extremely large chunk of coal and the rest was not soot but fine powdery coal dust. Then I asked, "What is that doing in the Carnival of Magic."

That is obvious. Coal brought us steel with the advent of coke for fuel. Coal brought mankind out of the dark ages with abundant energy for the first time. You can make almost anything out of coal: Electricity;

Plastic; Rubber; Gasoline; Oil; Medicine; Clothing; Transportation… You name it… coal is part and parcel with its creation. Politicians hate it but Coal is Magic.

Fid

Last night when I checked in with the Source I asked which project I should work on next. He said for me to move on to the next concession in the Carnival of Magic and to be sure that Innocence was with me. The next concession was sixty-nine.

The place was fantastic. We could see it from afar. The entire concession space was illuminated with what looked like the truncated end of a rainbow. The entire space shimmered in a myriad of rainbow colors. Tiny droplets of rain floated down like snow- flakes covering everything in dew. The entire space hummed with activity.

There were leprechauns everywhere, running around with their tiny little shovels, digging for gold.

They piled their little wheelbarrows full to the brim then dumped them in the center of the concession forming a growing mound. Every leprechaun hustled around, like crazy, except for one.

Standing on top of the pile of gold was a fat little leprechaun. We went over to the growing pile and asked the fat little leprechaun what was going on. He was shocked when I spoke Leprechaunese. I told him that Le Roy, the Leprechaun, was a close friend of mine.

I asked him what his name was and what he was doing standing on top of the pile of gold while everyone else was working so frantically. He told me that his real name was Benjamin and he was just fiddling around trying to avoid any real work. He said everyone called him Fid because he never did much of anything but just, fiddled around.

I turned to Innocence and said, "I guess there really is a pot of gold at the end of the rainbow." We stuffed as much gold into our pockets as we could carry, before the rainbow and the concession faded away.

Water Park

We could see concession seventy clearly from far away sitting in the middle of the desert all lit up and sparkling. There were no visitors there just Innocence and I. Like a miniature Las Vegas, water features were everywhere but, by comparison they were tiny in size, more varied and numerous. Water was doing things I never imagined were possible. Electric lights and whirring motors were twisting and tumbling in and out of the water. Ironically there was no spray or mist or even the smell of water. Where was the magic driving this fantastical menagerie. It certainly appeared to be some kind of magic. How else could you mix and match water with electricity, motion with lights and fountains without spray or dribble. The humidity was dry as a bone. Nothing added up until I tasted the water.

It wasn't water at all but a surrogate of some kind. It tasted like glycerin but looked like water. It felt like cornstarch, smooth and powdery. I was baffled. I looked all around for someone that might know something about what was going on here in this fantastic water park. Over in one corner there was a tiny little elfin man squatting down as if in hiding. I made my way over to where he was and asked if he knew anything about this concession. He stood up, smiled and said, "It's all just an illusion." Then, he vanished along with the entire water park.

War Horse

The next concession Innocence and I visited was number seventy-one. This concession like all of the others was a bit strange. In the middle of the concession's space there was a single central post with two long horizontal poles sticking out of it. At the end of each pole stood a horse all saddled up and ready to ride. The concession was set up so the tethered horses could walk around and around in a circle giving rides to children and I suppose to adults a horse ride as well. The central turnstile had additional holes in it for ten or twelve more poles for more horses. One of the horses was a young pony. The other was an old horse but very large by any standard.

There was a small man, perhaps a dwarf, at the entrance to this concession that ushered us in. He scanned our left hands before directing us over to get on a horse and start our ride around and around the turnstile. Innocence got up on the pony without too much difficulty. I took my time checking out the old horse. He had an insignia and a number branded on his right rear rump. It was an insignia of the Army. The numbers next to it were, one, nine, one, seven. This must have been a horse used to haul stuff a long time ago in very rough terrain where there were no roads. I checked his teeth. He still had most of them. I couldn't imagine what the point of riding an old horse around in a circle in the middle of the desert could possibly be.

As soon as my rear end hit the saddle, a shell exploded not twenty feet away. The old horse leaped into action, instinctively. We were traveling as fast as an old horse could move through deep mud with dead and dying men strewn all around us. Shells were whistling in and bursting all around us. Flames and smoke, shrapnel and flying mud, small arms fire and the rat-a-tat-tat of water-cooled machine guns filled the air. This was war, a trench war and we were in the thick of it, me and this old horse. I couldn't get out of there fast enough. As soon as my foot hit the ground we were back in the present, in a concession with two horses and a turnstile.

I immediately checked my horse for mud and blood, for injury from shrapnel and artillery shells. Nothing, there was nothing. This old war-horse was untouched.I was as clean as clean could be just as though nothing had even happened. I ran over to Innocence and checked him and his pony out. They were perfectly fine. I asked him what happened. He expounded on the wonderful adventure he and the pony had complete with a beautiful pasture, a lovely lake, swimming swans, a dense green forest, and a bubbling stream with flowers everywhere. I turned to the Dwarf and asked, "What's going on here." He replied, "They were merely sharing their stories with you. Horses don't talk, you know."

Sunny Day

I asked the Source what I should do next. He thought I should continue on to the next concession. When I went to get Innocence, he momentarily appeared as a monster. Then went back to his normal appearance, then as a monster again for a brief moment. He is supposed to be a spirit child. I had no idea what was going on with him. I asked the Source what might be happening. The Source told me to go on to the next concession which was number seventy-two with Innocence, so he and I visited concession seventy-two together last night. It was circumscribed by tall showers, which created a continuous ring all along the perimeter of the entire concession's space. The rows of showers were about four or five feet wide and twelve to fourteen feet high. Water was pouring down continuously in torrents like heavy rain. We entered the showers on the left side coming from the front of the concession. That side had a sign labeled ANIMOSITY. As we proceeded along the left side, the pure rainwater began to wash our clothes away. The back row of showers that we entered next had a big sign on it that read ANXIETY. It apparently was intended to wash away anxiety.

The far side had a large sign on it that read ANGER. Apparently it was supposed to wash away any anger that you harbored. When we reached the front side of the concession after being drenched on the left side, the backside and the right side of the string of showers we were completely clean but our clothes were all gone. When we entered the front of the concession it was a sunny day, not sunny from sunlight but mentally a sunny day. When we came out all of our clothes were neatly stacked and sparkling clean. Whatever evil spirits we might have harbored were now all washed away.

Ice Fairies

Innocence accompanied me to concession number seventy-three, last night. At first there seemed to be nothing there at all but after quite a while I could barely see something taking shape. It was outlined by several small, thin-lines of light. It was rectangular and covered the entire concession space. There were just a few lines. I really couldn't tell what it might be. The interesting thing was, Innocence saw the same things that I was seeing.

We went back several times, at least seven or eight, trying to figure out what was taking shape. Each time we returned there were more of these faint lines of light outlining something. Each time the rectangular outlined structure became taller and taller. The last time that I went, I was by myself. I left Innocence behind in a safe place so I could come down from above into the concession space.

It was hustling with activity. There were small characters about two or two and a half feet tall scurrying around everywhere positioning these strips of light. Standing, doing nothing, on a small hill like a pitcher's mound was a pudgy little fairy who's name turned out to be Cecil. By now this skeleton structure had windows but no doors and was ten stories high. I asked the fairy on the elevated mound what was going on. He said they were harvesting magic. That sounded ridiculous to me. The structure had no walls, no floors, no ceilings, and no doors.

Cecil told me that they separated the magic into different categories and bartered with them for other goods. Some of the magic was solid, some was powder and some were liquid for making magic potions. Each of the open sections trapped different kinds of magic. I know fairies have magic and use magic but I had no idea that they were capable of trapping magic and swapping it for other goods and services.

Cecil reinforced the claims that all magic originates from outside our own dimension, our own string number five. Black magic originates in string number three. Voodoo comes from string number two. Concession number seventy-three essentially was an entrapment device used to capture the many varied and unique forms of magic that abounds in the "Carnival of Magic". Cecil's home turned out to be Iceland. He said all the different kinds of magic were frozen for storage and taken back to Iceland for distribution.

Vaqueros

Concession number seventy-four was the next one that Innocence and I visited. This concession space was a large one, at least twice as wide and twice as deep as most. It was a veritable stockade completely surrounded with old railroad ties stood upright and bound together with leather, rope and bailing wire. There were horses and bulls, bucking broncos and barrel racing. This was a Rodeo and cowboys were displaying their skills that made them 'Vaqueros', which is the Spanish word for cowboys.

It was amazing what these seemingly men of iron could endure. Just watching them perform, you knew that there had to be some kind of magic behind every move. I certainly could not survive the many tortures they endured, seemingly unharmed.

To tame a bucking bronco or ride a raging bull, to trundle a squirming pig or rope a racing steer that surely takes magic, much more than I could ever muster.

Pastel Columns

When Innocence and I moved on to the next concession on our list of too do's, number seventy-five, it was easy to see lit up alone in the dark desert.

The entire concession space was surrounded with two overlapping rows of pastel columns. These were not ordinary columns. They were not painted but instead, they were illuminated from within by different pastel colors of light. The columns were eight or nine inches in diameter and appeared to be made of clear plastic or glass. They were separated from each other by a space of about four inches. The second row of pastel columns were positioned right against the first row, closing the four-inch gaps from behind. These columns were at least twelve to fourteen feet tall. The tops were wide open and the many colors of light spewed out from their tops creating a fantasy of dancing pastel colored light more delicate than the Aurora Borealis.

These tubes of light were evenly illuminated. I don't know how that effect was created. I have never seen anything quite like it. There was no top or roof on this concession. The front of the concession had a single entranceway. It wasn't a doorway. It was shaped like the top of a minaret, was wide open, and had sheer white gossamer thin curtains instead of doors. The entrance was almost seven-feet wide and seven-feet high at the center point. The interior was beautifully illuminated by all of the pastel columns of light. There was a central walkway of white marble about six-feet wide running the entire length of the concession. It was bisected by another pathway across the center running from side to side. The four spaces created by the two crossing marble pathways were filled with rectangular shaped pieces made of leather or some similar materials that were about eighteen-inches by twenty-six inches with rounded corners. If you stepped on them, they were not solid but semi-rigid. I had no idea what this place could possibly be.

We made several trips over there in an effort to comprehend what this concession was all about. On our third or fourth visit there, a strange creature came hustling out of the entrance and disappeared into the emptiness of the desert. I would describe it as a mixture of a human and a turtle. It was bipedal with two, more or less human, legs and arms but the neck and head were definitely turtle-like. The body resembled a carry-on suitcase.

When I went inside, I immediately noticed one of the rectangular pieces in the floor was missing. I thought, this is crazy, so then I asked Innocence what he saw when he entered this concession. To my surprise he said that the whole place was jammed full of suitcases. After much research I discovered what this place actually was. It was where lost luggage finally ends up. The suitcases that escape from here are spirited away by magic, the magic born of hope and prayer and wishful thinking of stranded travelers in strange lands without their luggage lost.

Amphitheater

Last night Innocence and I moved to the next concession on our list. It was number seventy-eight.

Needless to say it was an amphitheater in the middle of the desert. It wasn't half buried in the ground but on the contrary was completely above ground with only a single entrance into the arena. Since no one was there, I assumed that we or perhaps I was going to be the performer so I asked Innocence to take a front row seat while I took my place to strut upon the stage and perhaps make a fool of myself.

I got myself lost sometime during the process. It wasn't amnesia or perhaps it was. I lost track of time. When I finally looked up, Innocence was there, clapping away. I asked him what he had witnessed.

Innocence said that I moved deftly from one character to the next, acting out many different rolls in different languages and demonstrated specialized skills, some charming and smooth others brutal and violent. I was dancing, singing and cutting throats. I remember nothing. Perhaps these characters that I portrayed were the many and varied incarnations of my past and yes, even future lives yet unlived.

Piddle S. O. M.

Last night Innocence and I visited concession number seventy-nine. There didn't appear to be anything there but upon closer scrutiny we found a small blue-gray doorway about three by four inches protruding at a sixty-degree angle out of the ground.

It was an entranceway into a miniature tunnel that was complete with stairs and lighted interior.

I asked Innocence to guard the entrance while I shrank myself down to the size of small rat so that I was small enough to investigate this strange tunnel.

Once inside and the trap door closed I began to have second thoughts. There are lots of things that eat: small rats, like snakes and weasels, owls and hawks, raccoons and badgers, just to name a few. I didn't have any weapons. That was certainly a big concern.

I hadn't gone too deeply into that maze of tunnels before I ran into a mouse, not just any mouse but a magic mouse, a magic mouse named Michael who went by the name of Piddle, for Piddle was his nick name because he always just piddled around and he was the Son of Mousekin ergo S.O.M.

I ran into Piddle in the past. He was a mouse that liked to write. He wrote when he was happy. He wrote when he was sad. I wrote a story about him.

Monument

The next night Innocence and I investigated concession number eighty. It was easy to find. There, standing in the middle of the desert was the Washington Monument or was it a facsimile. It filled the whole concession space and towered high above everything. No one was around so Innocence and I walked in and checked it out. It looked authentic to me. When we reached the top and looked out I could see a really long ways in the clear dry desert air. There was nothing but pristine desert in every direction. I had no idea how the Washington Monument could have gotten here. Every detail about it seemed authentic to me. I asked Innocence what he thought about the monument and what he saw from high above. He too thought the monument was real and authentic but what he saw from the top was drastically different from what I observed. What he saw was the mall in Washington D.C. that surrounded the Washington Monument.

That was a clue to help me understand what this monument actually was. It was what is at the very heart of magic, Illusion. This whole thing was pure illusion, so real and believable that we climbed up to the top and each of us saw what we imagined.

Angus

When I went to 'The Place' to recharge I asked the Source if I should finish visiting the rest of the one hundred and seven concessions in the "Carnival of Magic" because I was down to about fifteen or so still to go. He said that I should start work on the "Twenty-six Strings". He suggested I start with our string, number five, because I could enter and exit that string anywhere and any time because I am familiar with reality in the Fifth String. So, instead of going on to the next concession, I exited our string number five right before the third string cut across it. The third string supposedly is the origin of 'Black Magic'.

When I exited string five I found myself in a dense forest. It wasn't a tropical jungle but more like a forest in a temperate climate. That's when I became concerned about where and when I actually was. I needed to find out where I was. I also wanted to know if I could get back to the place where and when I started. If I left this place looking for clues as to where I was, I didn't know if I could find my way back here or for that matter, anywhere else. I left there and went over to the next concession in the 'Carnival of Magic'. I needed a plan before striking out in an unfamiliar 'String' especially one touted as the source of all 'Black Magic'.

Concession eighty-one was identical to the dense forest I had just left in the 'Third String'. This was so bizarre I couldn't believe it. I was standing right next to this very same large tree. The dense vegetation was exactly the same. I needed to think this thing through, so I sat down in the middle of the forest and began to meditate on this situation.

An Elf appeared in front of me. He was almost four feet tall. I asked him who he was and what was going on with the same forest being here and there. He told me his name was Angus. He must be a Scottish Elf. We had a long discussion regarding this forest issue. He provided me with this explanation.

Angus explained the connections between the 'Third String', the 'Fifth String', the concession and himself. I of course had to ask if he were Scottish, with a name like Angus. He said that I had gone back in time along the 'Fifth String' until it encountered the 'Third String'. That happened to be on July 22nd, in the year 1115. The 'Third String' ran directly through our 'Fifth String'. That happened to be in the place that was or would become Scotland. He happened to be there in the forest at that moment in time so he was dragged along for the ride. He reminded me that all true magic originates in strings outside of our 'Fifth String'. Voodoo comes from the 'Second String', 'Black Magic comes from the 'Third String' and illusion originates in the 'Seventh String'. Just for good measure he threw in that the space ships we encounter come from the 'Ninth String'. That may prove useful in the future. He said that various strings cross each other all the time but the only time things ever happens is when the harmonics of both strings just happen to be identical. That is exceedingly rare. It was a long time ago. Angus got involved because he lives in the 'Fourth String', which happens to connect with both the third and the fifth strings forming a conduit through which things or people can pass through if everything lines up exactly.

Oil Lamp

Eighty-two was the next concession Innocence and I visited. We could see it from quite far away. It was a solid white structure that covered most but not all of the concession space. At first I thought it might be a miniature Mosque but once we were inside it was obviously not a religious structure but was used for domestic purposes. It was ornately decorated like a miniature palace but at the same time very Spartan with no bed, kitchen or bathroom. There were no furniture pieces per say, no table and chairs, no sofa, no closets and no place to do laundry. Those activities were obviously attended to outside.

In the middle of the central space beneath the domed roof was a silk rug, old but well preserved. It was intricately woven with strange patterns and symbols. There were gold tassels on both ends, all with an unusually large knot. Near one end sat a brass oil lamp. That looked to me like an accident waiting to happen so I went over to move it off of the rug.

As soon as I stepped on the rug the entire thing levitated off of the white marble floor. Perhaps this was Aladdin's fabled flying carpet and perhaps this brass oil lamp was the famous 'Magic Lamp' with the Genie inside. This is after all, 'The Carnival of Magic'.

I picked up the lamp and examined it carefully. It just looked old and tarnished and didn't seem to have any oil inside. The lid wouldn't come off. It was stuck on too tight for me to get it loose. I thought perhaps it unscrewed one way or the other. While I was messing with it a cloud of smoke whooshed out of the spout. It was dark gray and looked toxic to me. There was no Genie inside but there was a loud voice, "What is your wish?"

Innocence and I just looked over at each other.

Then we wished away.

Galveston

Last night, after we had checked out concession eighty-two, I went to 'The Place' to recharge my energy supply. While I was conversing with the 'Source' he said he wanted to show me something. At first it was a little distorted but then it became crystal clear. I was looking at the shore of a river or lake or some other body of water. There were three separate alcoves dug out of the vertical edge of land. It was obviously done mechanically, not naturally by erosion. The Source said, "Now that you are wealthy, I would like for you to put three Icons in these spaces." At the moment I certainly am not wealthy but I had just come from the "Oil Lamp" encounter where I asked the lamp to become rich so I took the request seriously and asked what kind of icons, like Saints or things like that.

The Source suggested saints of my choosing. I told the Source I was familiar with Saint Jude, the Patron Saint of lost causes and Saint Ignatius, the Patron Saint of soldiers. The Source suggested 'Mary' a well-recognized religious figure. I told the Source I had never met Mary so he introduced her to me. She was quite small and un-assuming. I asked her several loaded questions about her famous son, Jesus. I was surprised at some of her answers.

The Source then asked me if I had any idea where this place was. As usual, I had no Idea. The Source said, "Galveston".

Prairie Dog Town

The next concession on our list to visit was number eighty-three. When we got there I wasn't sure what to make of it. The place was totally devoid of any vegetation. Gopher holes were everywhere with mounds of dirt piled haphazardly all over the place and it smelled like a kid's dirty Gerbil cage. What kind of magic could be found in a mess like this?

There is probably just one way to find out... I'll have to become one of them.

I shape-shifted into a big, fat, lazy Prairie Dog.

The stench didn't seem so bad now. The tunnels looked inviting. The Town Folk welcomed me in like a long lost brother. Maybe being a prairie dog wasn't so bad. If the hawks don't catch you and the coyotes don't eat you and the snakes don't swallow you and the creek don't rise, who knows. There had to be some magic here somewhere but where do I start. If you really want to know something, ask an expert. So I did. I picked the smartest looking prairie dog and started digging. It's always best to start at the beginning.

All of these prairie dogs were related. That seemed like a bad idea to me. They're all vegetarians so that's a good start but this brother/sister thing has got to go. With all these prairie dogs in such a small space there is never enough food to go around and they have to travel too far afield to find anything worth eating. All that travel across open terrain will get you killed. The females seem to be the decision makers and all they want to do is make more prairie dogs. The males just wander around looking for a handout. They need to get organized. They need some direction. They need a plan. A good plan can work magic. I told them to all pair up with someone who wasn't a littermate and I would transport them pair by pair to places with water and plants and no prairie dogs. They all were hungry so they all agreed to my plan. I shape-shifted into an eagle and ferried them pair by pair all over the open prairie.

White Dove

Concession eighty-four was strange. It was a set of white canvas sails from a sloop sticking up out of the desert floor. The wooden mast, fore sail and main sails of heavy white canvas stuck straight up from the sand like the whole ship somehow was buried in the desert below, leaving only its mast and sails visible. We were very careful investigating this concession.

You never know what could happen, in the twinkle of an eye. I no more than touched the white canvas sail and we were on deck in the midst of heavy seas with gale force winds whipping the sails and drenching us with ice cold waves. With salt in our eyes, I lashed Innocence to the mast and tethered myself to the ship's wheel. Waves poured in from starboard, then from port. Before I knew it, waves ploughed over us from astern. I struggled to keep the bow headed into the waves.

What kind of magic could turn desert into sea?

That thin, fragile line between illusion and delusion had broken. We were prisoners of our own regrets.

How many times must this White Dove sail before she sleeps in the sand? The answer my friends, is blowing in the wind. The answers are blowing in the wind.

Velodrome

Before we visited concession eighty-five I asked Innocence how he thought we should approach it. We could drop down from above, circle it or go from the front or back or sides. It also makes a difference if we hold hands or not. Because so many strange things have happened to us, he thought we should approach from a side holding hands for safety and security, for we never knew what strangeness would await us.

The concession looked like normal desert at first but then it didn't look quite right. There seemed to be something odd superimposed upon the scene. If I released Innocence's hand it was definitely plain old desert but when I touched his hand again that strange imposition returned. I asked Innocence what he saw.

He said that when I held his hand there was a hazy something on the desert floor but when I released his hand the desert became a giant wooden bowl shaped structure that filled the entire space of the concession. I said, "Let me see what you see. Let me share your vision." Then, I could see clearly. It was a velodrome... a velodrome smack in the middle of the desert. Then I got it. I finally understood the magic in the 'Carnival of Magic'. It was "Trans-location". It was "Trans-migration" or perhaps more accurately, "Tele-portation" and "Tele-migration". Not only is time fluid but place as well is also fluid. That is how these concessions come and go to different places, in different times as if by 'magic'.

Telephone Pole

When Innocence and I visited concession number eighty-six the only thing we saw there was a telephone pole, right in the middle of the space reserved for that concession. It was an antique telephone pole, small, short, with only one cross piece and two small wires, one attached on each side of the crosstie, supported by small glass insulators. The old wood spike-marked pole was still brown but had lost all of its creosote smell. The two wires were strung straight out horizontally from the crosstie held taught as if by some invisible attachments but both wires ended abruptly mid-air at the edge of the concession.

We walked around and around the small pole. We were trying to figure out what the point of it was. Innocence went up to it and put both of his small hands onto it. That wood pole instantly turned into a tall modern cell-phone tower. It still made no sense at all to me. I continued to explore the entire concession space. I heard the un-mistakable ring of a cell-phone. There in front of me on the ground was a generic looking cell-phone. I stooped and picked it up and said, "Hello."

The voice on the other end asked, "Is this Michael." I wasn't born yesterday so I said, " Who may say is calling?"

The voice answered, " Why this is God. We have a special offer for you today, three for the price of one. I'm sure you wouldn't want to miss out on this special. You are Michael, aren't you?"

I got it. I hung up the cell phone. The antique old telephone pole with its skinny, bare wires were from my past, from my time. The shiny new cell tower was modern, up to date, omnipresent and omnipotent filled with endless truths and delights.

The latest, greatest, new cell-phone can track your every move, anticipate your every desire, fill your mind with non-sense and steal all your time.

Piggy-Man

Concession number eighty-seven was another strange one. We held hands going over there. When we arrived we saw a single, fat pig in the middle of the concession's space that was covered with dry powdery dirt. Surrounding this space, there was a small, low curb separating it from the desert outside. The pig appeared to be about eighteen months old and weighed perhaps on the short side of two hundred pounds. Its pink skin showed through its short white and black hair. There was nothing else there but that fat little pig.

We stayed there for a while trying to figure out what the point of the pig was, before leaving. When we returned we were no longer holding hands. What I saw now was a much larger pig sitting in the middle of the concession space filled with white sand that was surrounded by a single strand of razor wire stretched tightly, floating, suspended about two feet above the sand. By comparison, Innocence said that what he saw was a fat Sumo Wrestler sitting Buddha- style on a small mound of beach sand. There was no longer a low curb or razor wire surrounding the concession space, just a smooth transition into desert.

I proceeded to go out onto the sand and sat down face to face with the pig. I stared deep into its eyes, one was a bright red and the other was sapphire blue. I shape-shifted into a pig. The pig morphed into a Sumo Wrestler. Later, I asked Innocence what he had seen. He said that the Sumo Wrestler and I morphed into a

Buddha, sitting on a mound of sand.

My chest was rocking back and forth, back and forth. I checked my pulse. It was slow and steady but I was rocking, rocking, rocking to the beat of the clock tic…tock…tick…tock…tic…tock, moving closer, from eight to seven to six inches away, closer and closer until the space had vanished. Now we were one, the pig and I together, sitting on the sands of time.

Double Eagle

Eighty-eight was the next concession Innocence and I visited. That leaves eight more to go. The place was weird from the start. Standing alone in the middle of the desert was a rocky alcove with sparse vegetation reminiscent of a mountaintop high above the tree line. There were the trunks of two dead trees standing next to each other. A giant eagle's nest was suspended between the branches of the two trees. A Bald Eagle was perched in the tree to the left. A Red Eagle was perched in the tree to the right. Bald Eagles and Red Eagles are incompatible. They will fight to the death. I asked Innocence to tell me what he saw.

He said there was a beautiful Alpine meadow with luscious green grass, strewn with colorful spring flowers surrounding two magnificent trees, a White Pine on the left and a Blue Spruce on the right, both filled with bustling forest animals and chirping birds. That was not what I saw, so I moved into the eagle's nest facing the Bald Eagle. I asked the eagle if it were a shape-shifting Indian Medicine Man. It said no and morphed into a pine tree. It was a shape-shifting tree spirit. I turned to the Red Eagle and asked if it were a shape-shifting Indian Medicine Man. It said no and morphed into a spruce tree. It also was a shape-shifting tree spirit. It never occurred to me that tree spirits could shape-shift into animals and other forms. I asked the tree spirits how Innocence could easily see them in their true form when I could not. They reminded me that Innocence was a spirit child who embodied the innocence of a child while I was a shape-shifting 'Druid' seeking to understand the nature of magic, which dwells only in the innocent mind of a child.

Later when I went to 'The Place' to replenish my energy supply the Source smiled and said," You're getting it. You're finally getting it.

Speed-Bowl

Concession eighty-nine was a speed-bowl. What is a speed-bowl you might ask? That's what I called it.

So, let me describe my take on what I encountered and share with you my understanding of what it does.

1) It consisted of two parts, a bowl and a ring.
2) It has therapeutic and analytic value.
3) It introduces the final element of magic.

The bowl was the size of the entire concession. It was composed of half a sphere. It could be tilted and

175

could be rotated clock-wise or counter clock-wise at any specific speed. The ring was attached to the opening of the bowl and could rotate around the edge of the bowl separately or remain stationary while the bowl itself rotated in either direction. The ring had two adjustable tubes or handrails that ran straight across the center of the ring like railroad tracks. It could move up or down so that a person's feet could be in contact with the inside surface of the bowl while their hands could hold on to the two handrails. There was also a suspensory safety cable and harness to secure the participant during movement of the bowl. The participant wears boots similar to roller-blades with one exception. The rollers are not fixed in line but each roller swivels independently of the other rollers like the casters do on an office swivel chair.

Therapeutic value lies in returning an injured limb to its normal function as quickly and safely as possible while minimizing undesirable twisting and torqueing of the healing appendage and harmonizing beneficial gravitational effects and re-establishing normal balance. The analytical values lie in the ability to accurately monitor and manipulate the parameters associated with the healing and well-being of patients.

This device can also be utilized to break the bonds between gravity and directional orientation. We are conditioned from birth to sense gravitational forces as 'down' and the opposite as 'up'. In space there are no 'ups' or 'downs'. By disassociating visual cues from gravitational cues the normal bonds between physical reality and non-ordinary reality are altered. Magic is non-ordinary reality at its core.

Historically Sorcerers would hang novitiates suspended from trees for days to loosen their grip on physical reality and engage non-ordinary reality, the world of the sorcerer.

Tomb Stone

I was shocked when I saw concession number ninety. Innocence and I were holding hands but I was still shocked by what I saw. The whole concession was a huge rectangular hole in the ground with a giant white marble tombstone sticking up in back of it. The top was round. The message was clear, R.I.P.

There was no name on it. I assumed it would be my grave. We always assume the worst. That seems to be human nature, "Always think the worst". I asked Innocence what he saw. He said he saw a wide muddy river with families standing on the other side, old men, children, women holding tiny babies. I asked the Source for some kind of explanation. He told me what the point of the grave at concession ninety was.

He said, "Today is the seventy-fifth anniversary of the 'Battle for Iwo Jima'. More than seven thousand American soldiers perished here and close to twenty thousand Japanese soldiers died as well. It was brutal hand-to-hand combat."

I was there. I could see Mount Suribachi in the

distance as plain as day. The Source said my task now was to liberate all the remaining souls still stranded here after seventy-five years. As we traversed back and forth over the caves and battlegrounds, the lost souls poured fourth beginning long-delayed journeys to rejoin their respective families.

This reminded me of the magic in 'Flanders Fields'.

Flanders Fields

I was walking with the Source last night. He asked me if I knew where we were. I told him that I had no idea where we were. He said, "In Flanders Fields". As we walked along wisps of smoke puffed out of the ground and shot up into the night sky. He asked if I knew what all those wisps of smoke were. Again I told him that I had no idea. The Source said they were the spirits of soldiers who died in World War I. He said that he had been here many times encouraging these many departed young soldiers to come out from hiding in their respective shallow graves but none would ever do so because they felt guilty and were too afraid of what the Source might do to them, to leave the safety of their respective graves but when I accompanied the Source, they quickly came forth and departed for their unknown futures because they felt safe in my presence. I have no idea why that would be the case. After the Source departed, leaving me alone in Flanders Fields, I continued to walk the entire area where all of these spirits have remained for the past hundred years. With my passing they continued to pour forth from beneath the green grasses, where poppies once grew, in Flanders Fields.

I chanced upon the grave of one, Tyler Moore, dead by age seventeen. That seemed very young to me to come to the end of one's life so violently. I was drawn to this particular grave by a sense of great sadness and futility. As I contemplated Tyler's passing at such a young age I sensed movement out of the corner of one eye. I asked perchance could that be the ghost of Tyler Moore. The answer came back as a yes. He lied to get into the army and died not as the hero he envisioned but as a gut-shot kid sorrowful and fearful of death's coming. He never forgave himself for the untold sadness his pointless demise inflicted upon his mother and his friends. I assured him that they were all now, long since dead and buried and surely awaiting his arrival where they would rejoice at his homecoming. Excited he departed, last of all in leaving Flanders Fields, where poppies once grew.

Candle Lights

Innocence and I visited concession ninety-one, last night. The entire concession was jammed pack full of people all holding up an unlit candle in a glass jar high above their bowed heads. Nothing was in color. Everything was in shades of gray. These were like the ones you light at church and place in front of a religious statue. This made no sense to me.

We hung around there for a while but nothing was happening so we left and were going to go back later. I had another project that I was working on. I was looking for an individual by the name of Kurt Nacionales. He was a mentally disturbed young man who had apparently attempted to commit suicide in his parent's home but had not been successful. I became involved with this project when the young couple that rented that house were having problems with spirits or ghosts. They asked me to get rid of whatever was causing problems for them in that rental property.

When I went there a few days ago it was a little after one o'clock in the morning. This fairly large young man came down the hall towards me. He didn't look or behave like a ghost. He appeared to be in his late twenty's or early thirty's. His hair was dirty blond with a tinge of red, a little on the long side and wavy but not quite curly. I thought he might be Kurt. I tried to get his attention and called him by name but he rushed right by me and went into the bathroom and was rummaging around. I came to get rid of whatever was there so I stuffed him into this leather bag I carry that puts things into suspended animation. When I started dragging him outside I discovered he was quite heavy. That meant he wasn't a ghost or a spirit. He had to be something that had physical properties and could obviously interact with physical things like a poltergeist or a 'Freddy Kruger' or some other strange thing I wasn't familiar with. I didn't know what to do with it so I took it home and dumped it in my front yard under an apple tree. I made several inquiries in an attempt to learn more about what I was dealing with but to no avail. I was advised to, "let sleeping dogs lie."

When I finally encountered Kurt Nacionales, I knew immediately what happened. Somehow before, during or after the suicide attempt Kurt's body had been taken over by a demon of some kind. I think it is a wraith. Its glowing yellow eyes and shadowy presence engulfed what remained of Kurt's physical body. What I previously encountered in the hall and now held in a leather bag on ice was the fragmented body and soul of Kurt. So what I did was to force the 'Cross of Palmero' onto his forehead. He writhed in pain and fell backwards. I then forced the mystic 'Celtic Cross' onto his forehead and as he stumbled backwards, I hurtled a psychic explosive device at him. When it exploded, Kurt fell limp to the floor and the demon departed.

I took Kurt's limp body and stuffed it into the leather bag where the rest of his fragmented soul was, then pushed the bag with both parts of him through the 'Door of No Returns' where the separate parts would be reunited. From there I took the bag with Kurt still inside and returned to concession ninety-one. As I descended down onto the concession I dumped the bag. All of the candles in all of the glass jars lit up at once. All of their prayers for Kurt had been answered. He flew off into the physical world and is now alive and well, no longer insane, and no longer possessed by demons.

I asked Innocence what he had seen. He told me that when we first arrived, the throng of people all held up white crosses high in the air with their heads bowed in prayer. When their prayers were answered each cross became a yellow flower and all the flowers flew up into the air and coalesced into a handsome young man, a man named Kurt Nationales.

There must be magic in lighted candles and fervent prayer and yellow flowers.

Spirit Dancers

Last night, Innocence and I visited concession number ninety-two. For me there was an oval path around the inside of the concession. It was a little more than four feet wide but not quite five feet wide.

I think closer to fifty-five or fifty-six inches wide. The surface of the path looked like weathered asphalt but it felt more like ground up old rubber tires that are used to make tennis-courts. The center was filled with white sand. The outer edge was pristine desert.

Innocence said he saw an oval pathway in the midst of a meadow in an Alpine forest with a background of coniferous trees. We hung around there for half an hour before we took off because nothing was happening there. A few hours later I returned alone.

Out of a slit in the pathway emerged full-sized Kachinas. They weren't dolls but were human-sized Kachina Spirits. One by one they emerged from the earth and paraded around the oval pathway. They were all identical Kachina Spirits. I counted them. There were seventeen of them in all. I had no idea what they were for or what they represented so I had to ask. It turns out that they were all my Kachina Spirit Dancers one for each of the lives I have lived.

When a Sorcerer's Death comes, it can be held at bay while the sorcerer dances their dance, which embodies all their experiences and accomplishments in that life. I have seventeen Kachinas, so my death will be held at bay while I dance the seventeen dances that embody my seventeen journeys through life.

Back Door

The next concession was number ninety-three. This one like many of the others was very odd. The whole space was filled with geometric sections like slices in a loaf of bread. Each slice had a unique shape. Each slice was about twenty-eight inches thick and seven to nine feet high. Each slice or segment ran the entire length of the concession. The ends of the slices were mostly vertical but the tops were cut into squares and triangles Each one was different. The segments were aligned next to each other across the front of the concession. It was like a loaf of bread that had been sliced long ways instead of crossways.

I walked down the front of concession ninety-three counting the segments. There were twenty-six of them.

That suggested to me that they might be associated with the twenty-six strings of reality. I fiddled around with the segment ends and managed to get some of them open. They were doorways. There was a passage behind each door. Each passageway led somewhere. I think each door was a back door. I think each passageway leads to a different reality, a different string. I think these doors are the back doors to the twenty-six strings of reality. That is what everybody looks for. That is what everyone wants, a "Back Door" to everything.

Mirror Mirror

Concession ninety-four was easy to find but complicated to understand. For me, the entire space of the concession had been graded clean. Nothing was left of the desert or desert vegetation, just dirt, plain dry dirt. I asked Innocence what he saw. Innocence said that he saw plain desert completely devoid of any vegetation as though every plant had been surgically excised, leaving the desert itself completely undisturbed. I didn't get it. There was no one around. We waited there quite awhile but no one ever came.

Several hours later we returned. I went out into the middle of the space, sat down and meditated on the missing landscape. It made absolutely no sense to me. Each concession is supposed to have some kind of magic associated with it. There was nothing here. I was looking for something that wasn't there. What could that possibly be? Finally my mind was clear. Finally I was in the moment. My mind was open to anything. I opened my eyes and started to get up. There on the ground right in front of me was a mirror, a hand mirror. I picked it up and looked into it.

I wasn't there. The missing desert around me was present there in the mirror but I was not. I showed the mirror to Innocence. He looked into it and he wasn't there either but the missing desert vegetation had returned or perhaps was never actually gone. This mirror must have powerful magic. Were we seeing the desert past, before we came or were we seeing the desert future, after we are no longer here or are we seeing the desert as it should always be ideally? Were we seeing reality as it was, as it will be or as it should be, all without our even being there?

Blue Agave

For this particular concession, Innocence and I both approached from high above. As we came down it appeared to stand out from the surrounding desert. It was entirely filled with Blue Agave that is known as Agave Tequilana because that is what tequila is made from. Row after row of Blue Agave plants filled up the entire concession space. All around the base of each agave plant were baby agave plants, known as 'pups'. The tall stalks rising from each plant were filled with seeds. The variety of Agave that are common here is

Agave Americana we call them 'century plants' even though they don't live a hundred years. They live a very long time and flower only once then they die. Before they die they send off several underground shoots producing baby agave plants. They also produce seeds from their tall central stalks, which are six to eight feet tall. The flowers are very large and edible as well as the stalk itself, if taken early before it matures and becomes leather hard. The stalk tastes like green beans. It is even the same green color as string beans. I asked Innocence if he saw what I saw.

Innocence said that he saw row upon row of very small Blue Agave plants all lined up like little soldiers. He saw them at the beginning of their long lives. I saw them at the end of their lives. When we held hands, we both saw them at their zenith in full bloom displaying their gigantic white flowers. We saw magic in the circle of life for the Blue Agave.

Elliot

Innocence and I were heading for the last of the one hundred and seven concessions. It was number ninety-six. There were times when I thought we would never finish seeing them all but here we were. The place was empty. It was desert, plain desert. We walked around. We sat down. We waited. We were ready to leave when a very small creature appeared.

I wasn't sure what it was. It was larger than a

leprechaun. It was smaller than a gnome. It wasn't a fairy. It wasn't a dwarf and certainly was not a small child. It seemed too small for an elf and its eyes were too big. I asked why it was here. The small creature said it was a midget Elf and it assisted the caretaker of the 'Carnival of Magic' by providing any magic that was needed during its 'day to day' and 'place to place' operations. When I asked for a name, it said, "Guess."

So I tried every name I could think of but finally gave up in the end. It said, "Elliot" and that seemed to fit.

He first got his table, his table for two.
Sat down behind it and offered us Brew.
I asked for lemonade, sweetened not pink.
Innocence asked for some Kool-Aid to drink.

He complained that we had damaged a few.
So the other concessions he withdrew.
He allowed us to see them one at a time,
until we went through the whole entire line.

With the snap of his fingers, one or two
Concession ninety-six came into view.
Now it was high time to finish our task.
So, no more questions, don't even ask.

This concession was a combination of all kinds of games: A ring-toss; A duck shoot; A bell ringer; A baseball throw; A fortune teller and A coin toss.

The prizes were cheesy and the carnies were sleazy. This whole concession was straight from the forties, matching my memories to the smallest detail.

With the snap of his fingers and the click of his tongue the entire 'Carnival of Magic' sprang back to life. The center space down the middle was now filled with food stands; hot dogs, hamburgers, french-fries, popcorn, cotton candy, corn dogs, soda pop and yes, best of all, even beer.

Magic Wand

Last night when I asked the Source if there was anything he wanted to show me, any place he wanted to take me, any place he wanted me to go, any thing he wanted to tell me or anything he wanted me to do. He said it was time for me to get my wand. I chose to go through the 'Black Door' to the 'Wand Shoppe'. It was a very Medieval looking place with cobble stone streets, narrow and crowded, shops jammed next to each other, oil lamps, no electricity, no autos, only wagons and liveries and funny-dressed people. The inside of the place reminded me of a curios shop. The shopkeeper was standing behind a tall wood counter. Behind him there was a wall of cubicles. The cubicles on the left half of the wall, were filled with all kinds of wands. The cubicles on the right side of the wall were all completely empty. He asked me what I was looking for. I told him a magic wand, one a magician could use.

He said the wands on my left side were all for sorcerers. The cubicles on my right side were for magician's wands. The cubicles there were all empty. He directed me to a small stack of parchment papers approximately two inches by four inches in size on the counter next to an ink pen sticking up out of a bottle of sepia-ink and a shaker to sprinkle powder over what you had written to make the ink dry faster. He told me to write my name on one of the parchment papers. After I wrote my name on the parchment paper he wanted me to sprinkle it with dusting powder. When I did the parchment burst into flames and burned up. At the same time a magic wand appeared in one of the cubicles. The end of the wand glowed with a strange light. The shopkeeper said, "That is your wand. You created it with your own magic. You and only you can use the magic held within it". I thanked the shopkeeper for his assistance and asked how much it would be. He said, "Magic is free for the taking. Use it wisely or not at all."

Glossary

Blue Agave Also called a century plant because they live so long. The Mexican Blue Agave is used to make tequila. It is a giant agave plant that grows in harsh climates of the Sonoran Desert.

Eyes Sorcerers' are black as coal. Wizards' eyes glow fiery red. Magicians' eyes are sapphire blue.

High Stepping This is a modification of speed walking where you pick your feet up very high with each step.

Island of Vishnu The island where Vishnu resides. This place is where the universe was created and is sustained.

Kartikeya is the six-headed God. He was brother of Ganesha and second son of Shiva and Parvati. He carries a spear in one hand and blesses worshipers with his other hand. His six heads stand for his six virtues and allows him to see in every direction to see danger coming and to fend off the six demonic vices: Kaama (sex); Krodha (anger); Lobha (greed); Moha (passion); Mada (ego); Matsarya (jealousy).

Naigamesha is one of the forms that Kartikeya takes. He is the god of war and is depicted with the head of a goat.

Speed Walking A technique used by a sorcerer, magician or Buddha tomove rapidly from one place to another by walking not on the surface of the ground but at some height above it.

Vantage Point That point from which one can view simultaneously the Event Horizon, the past Event Horizon that gave birth to it but also the possibilities and probabilities associated with specific that event.

Voodoo of Louisiana origin.Haitian Vodou is a syncretic religion based on West African Vodun. Practioners are known as Vodouists. They believe in a supreme creator, Bondye.

Yo Kai The spirit of a dearly departed person that hascombined with the spirit of an animal or inanimate object or thing that also is no longer living.They were created or connected by a traumatic death.Each YoKai acquires a unique name and each YoKai has special gifts or powers.They are invisible but create all kinds of challenges and influence our every day lives.

Books by Dr. Mayo

The trilogy 'Coincidental Journey', 'Untold Story', & 'Wizardling', are about Lucid Dreaming, Dream-walking, Shape-shifting, Sorcery, Wizardry, Magic, Time Travel and the power of Illusion.

'Coincidental Journey'   Copyright 2015
   ISBN # 978-1-940985-16-9
   Completed in 2015; awaiting publication.
'Untold Story'   Copyright 2016
   ISBN # 978-1-940985-42-8
   Completed in 2016; awaiting publication.
'Wizardling'   Copyright 2017
   ISBN # 978-1-940985-73-2
   ISBN # 978-1-7345741-3-5 e-book
   Published and released in: April 2019
'Robin'   Copyright 2018
   ISBN # 978-1-940985-55-8
   ISBN # 978-1-7345741-5-9 ebook
   A 268 page book of Elizabethan poetry.
   Published and released in: April 2018
'Oracle'   Copyright 2018
   ISBN # 978-1-940985-95-4
   ISBN # 978-1-7345741-6-6 ebook
   Published and released in: December 2018
' Vision Quest'   Copyright 2019
   ISBN # 978-1-7345741-0-4
   ISBN # 978-1-7345741-1-1 e-book
   Completed in 2019. Published February 2020
'Art of Magic'   Copyright 2020
   ISBN # 978-1-7345741-2-8
   ISBN # 978-1-7345741-4-2 e-book
   Completed in April 2020. Published July of 2020

'Saving Seventeen'   Copyright 2020
    ISBN # 978-1-7345741-7-3
    ISBN # 978-1-7345741-8-0   ebook
    Completed in May of 2020, awaiting publication.
'Star Quest: Navigator'   Copyright 2020
    ISBN # 978-1-940985-74-9
    This book evaluates several exoplanets located
    within the habitable zones of their star system
    for intelligent life and Human habitability.
    Completion date slated for 2020.

Current Projects

'Twenty six strings' The exploration of the twenty six
    separate strings that comprise string theory.
'1937' Is about our future conflict with artificial
    intelligence. Its completion date is pending.
'I, Druid' The theme of this book unites all of the books.
    Its completion date is pending.
'Neptune' The search for intelligent life on Neptune
    and its thirteen moons is currently being researched.
    Its completion date is pending.
'No-vas: The Lost Continent' It is currently being
    researched. Its completion date is pending.

About Dr. Mayo

Dr. Mayo was born in Tucson, Arizona where he maintains a private practice located in the heart of Tucson. His practice is limited to the treatment of children and special needs patients.

Dr. Mayo obtained the pictures for the front and back covers of this book courtesy of PIXABAY.

Notes

Notes

Notes

Notes

CPSIA information can be obtained
at www.ICGtesting.com
Printed in the USA
FSHW020355071221
86599FS

9 781734 574128